HUMAN BODY

An Hachette UK Company
www.hachette.co.uk

First published in Great Britain in 2017 by Bounty Books,
a division of Octopus Publishing Group Ltd
Carmelite House, 50 Victoria Embankment
London EC4Y 0DZ
www.octopusbooks.co.uk

Copyright © Octopus Publishing Group Ltd 2017

Edited and designed by Anna Bowles and Perfect Bound Ltd

All rights reserved. No part of this work may be reproduced or utilized in any form or by any means, electronic, or mechanical, including photocopying, recording or by any information storage and retrieval system, without the prior written permission of the publisher.

ISBN 978 0 7537 3233 5

Printed and bound in China

1 3 5 7 9 10 8 6 4 2

Publisher: Lucy Pessell
Designer: Lisa Layton
Editor: Natalie Bradley
Proofreader: Jane Birch
Administrative Assistant: Sarah Vaughan
Production Controller: Sarah Kulasek-Boyd

Artworks created by Perfect Bound Ltd

COLOUR + LEARN
HUMAN BODY

MORE THAN 200 PAGES OF FASCINATING FACTS + COLOURING

CONTENTS

Your Body 6
Your Organs 8

PART 1: CONTROL CENTER 10

The Brain 12
Your internal computer

Parts of the Brain 14
Which bit controls what?

Left and Right Brain 16
Lefties and righties

Nerves 18
Signals to the brain

The Nervous System 20
A network of nerves

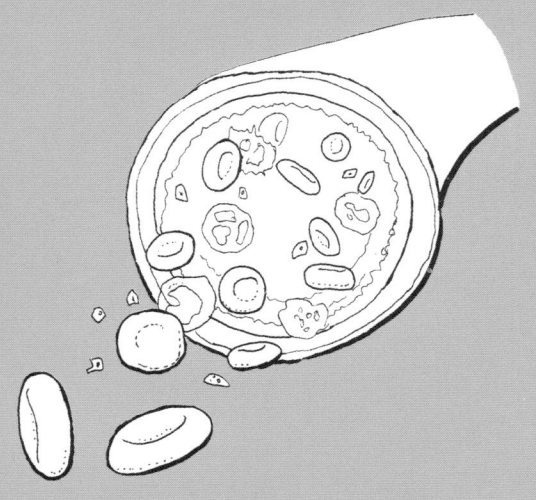

PART 2: HEART AND LUNGS 22

What is Blood? 24
The fluid that feeds your organs

The Heart 26
Pumping blood around your body

Veins and Arteries 28
Blood vessels

Capillaries 30
The tiniest vessels

Why Do We Breathe? 32
The need for air

How Do We Breathe? 34
Taking in air

The Lungs 36
Processing air

Inside the Lungs 38
Getting oxygen to the blood

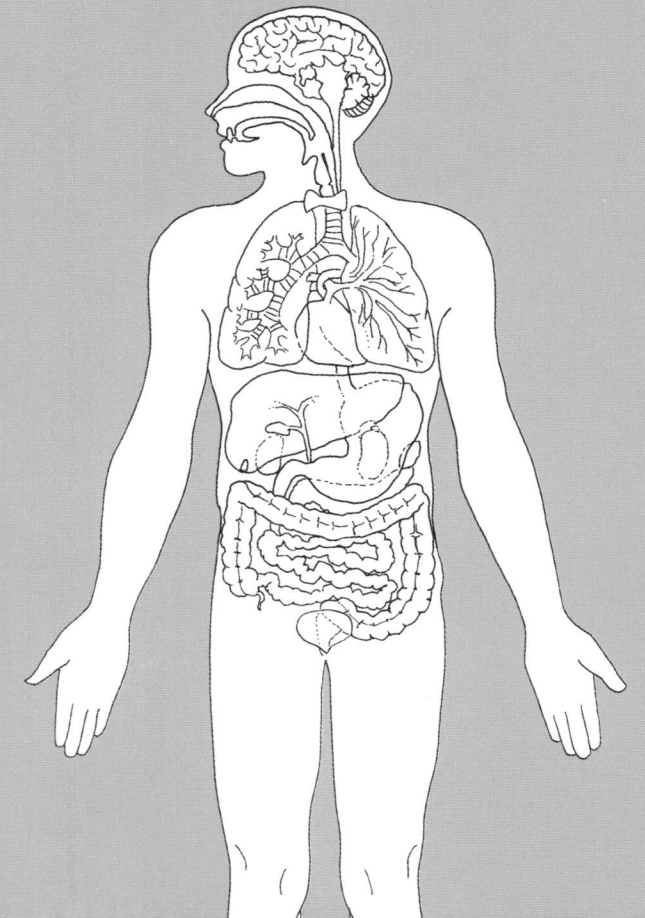

PART 3: EATING AND DIGESTION 40

Teeth 42
Readying food for digestion

Inside a Tooth 44
The hardest part of the body

Digestion 46
Turning food into fuel

The Mouth 48
Where digestion begins

The Throat 50
Breathing and swallowing

Food 52
The essentials to survive

Vitamins 54
Vital chemicals

Food's Journey 56
From mouth to anus

The Stomach 58
Absorbing nutrients

The Intestines 60
Food's onward journey

The Liver 62
Making chemicals

The Kidneys 64
Cleaning the blood

PART 4: SENSES 66

The Eyes 68
How we see

The Ears 70
How do we hear?

The Nose 72
How do we smell?

The Tongue 74
How do we taste?

Touch 76
How do we feel?

PART 5: BONES 78

What is Bone? 80
What keeps us standing?

Skeleton 82
The structure of the body

The Spine 84
The backbone

The Joints 86
How we bend and flex

The Muscles 88
How we move

Tendons 90
Connecting muscles to bones

Hands and Feet 92
Gripping and Walking

Arms and Legs 94
Your limbs

YOUR BODY

You are one of the most amazing systems on Earth. You contain billions of cells, thousands of miles of blood vessels, and a human brain—a thinking machine far more complex than any computer.

Turn over the page to see your whole body!

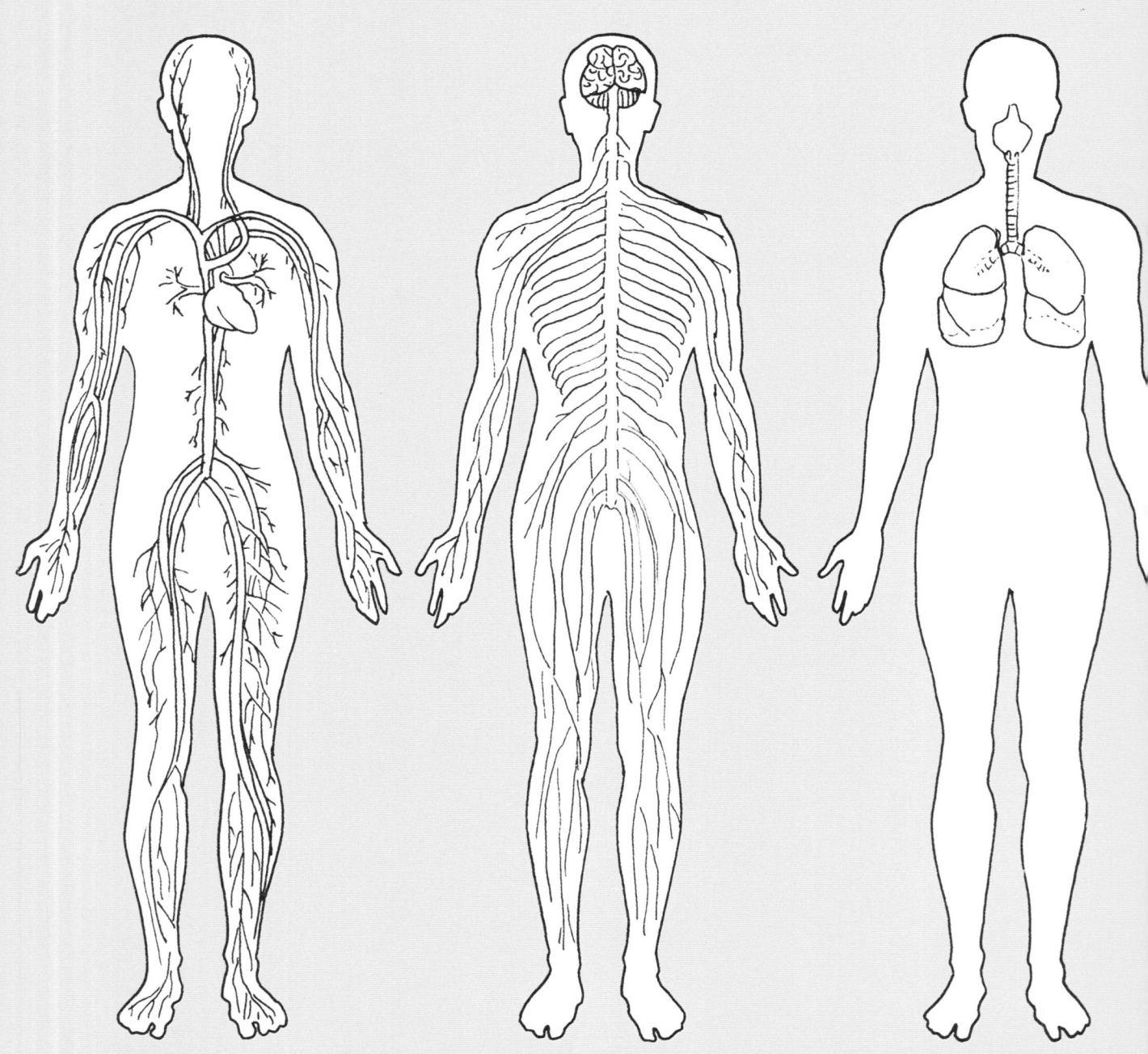

QUICK FACTS

The human body has more than 10 trillion **CELLS**.
Written in full, that's 10,000,000,000,000.

During an average lifetime (70 years) the heart **BEATS** 2.5 billion times.

Around 95 per cent of cells in the human body are **BACTERIA**.

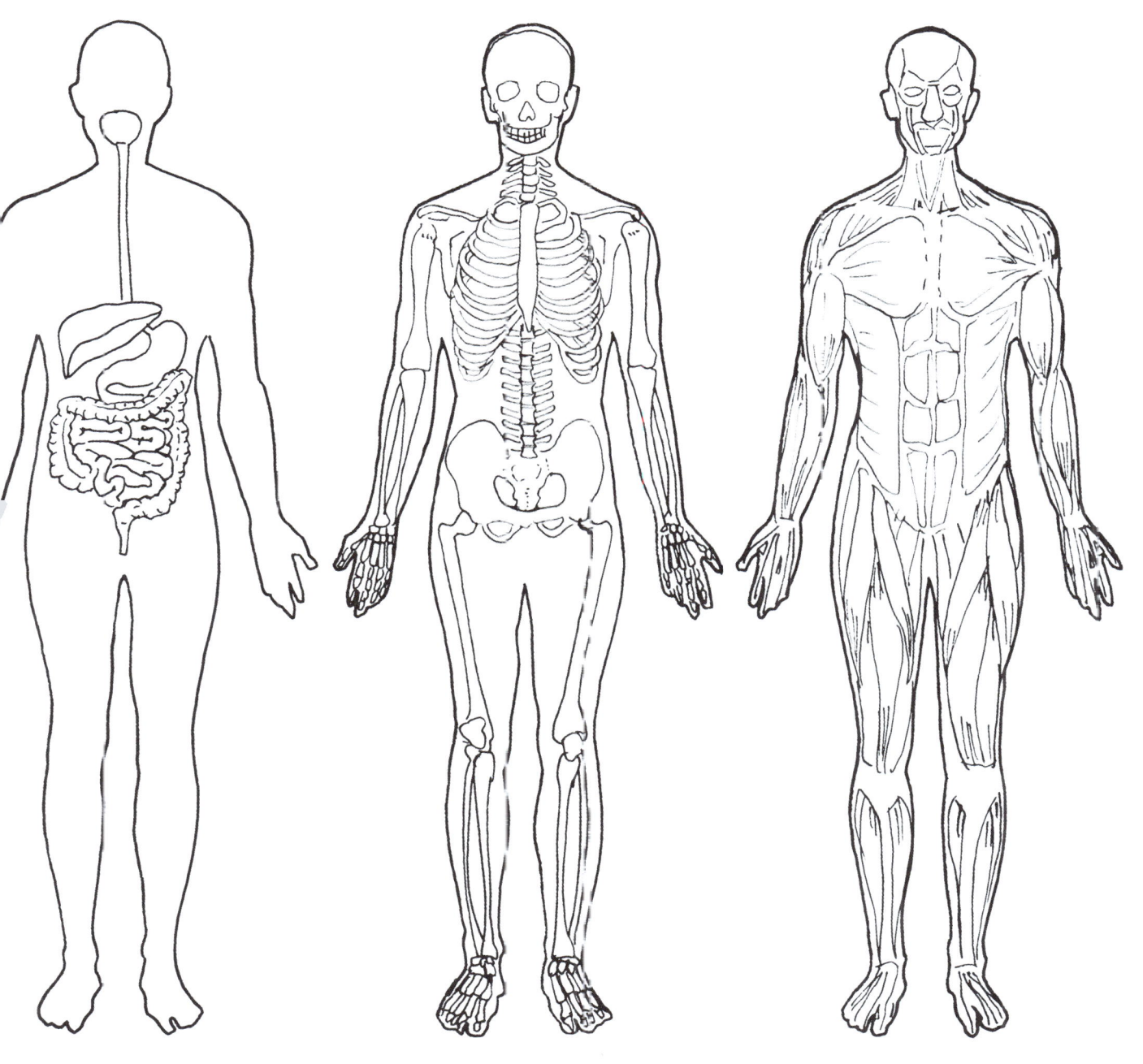

YOUR ORGANS

Every organ in the human body works as part of a team, to keep you going and make you who you are.

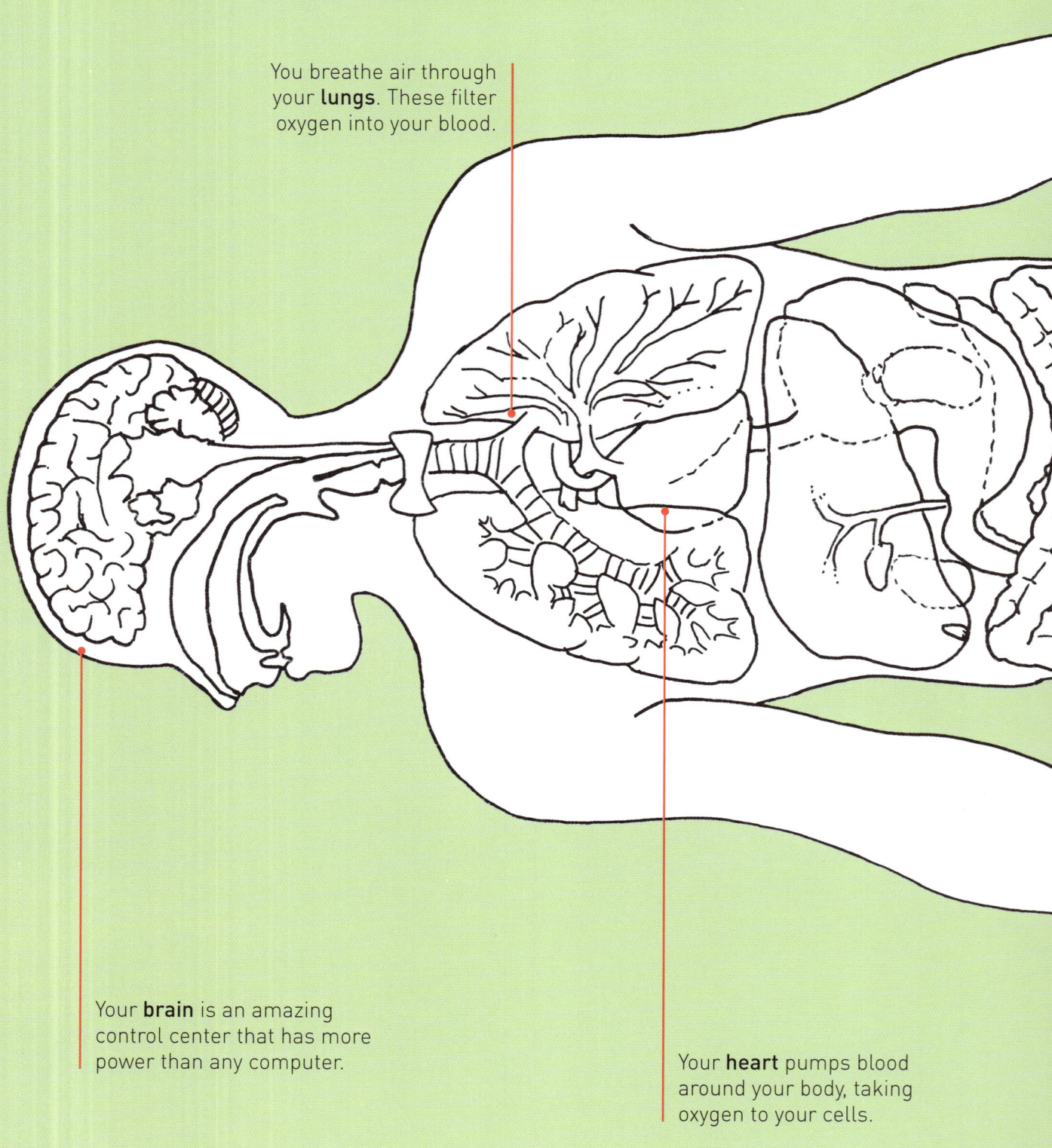

You breathe air through your **lungs**. These filter oxygen into your blood.

Your **brain** is an amazing control center that has more power than any computer.

Your **heart** pumps blood around your body, taking oxygen to your cells.

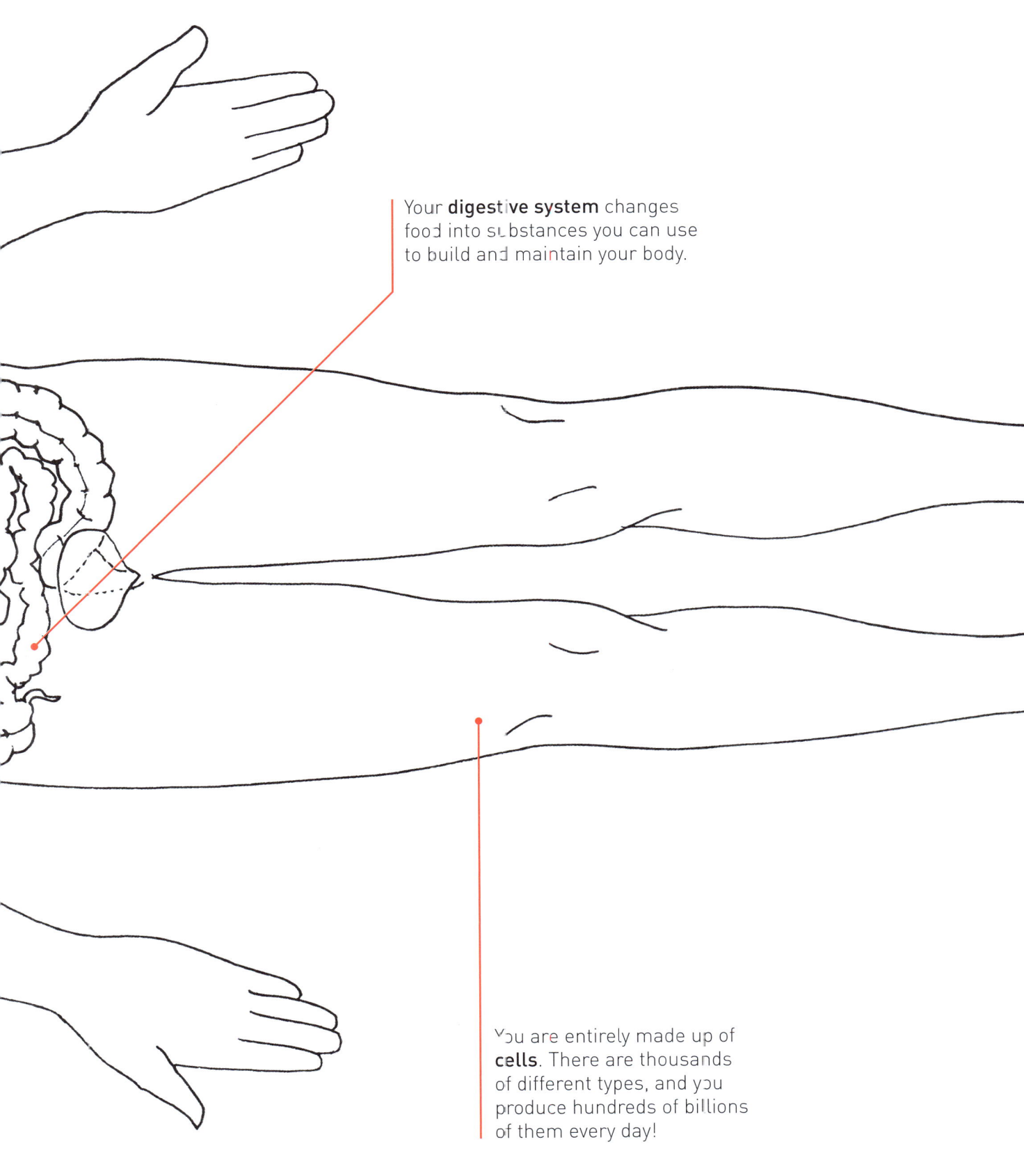

Your **digestive system** changes food into substances you can use to build and maintain your body.

You are entirely made up of **cells**. There are thousands of different types, and you produce hundreds of billions of them every day!

CONTROL CENTER

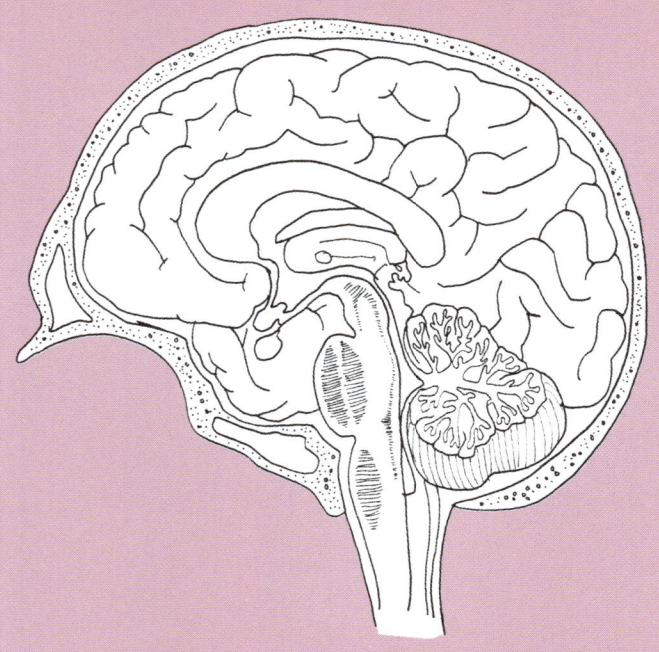

THE BRAIN

The brain is the body's control center. It coordinates all the messages that pass through the nervous system, giving us the ability to learn, reason, and feel. It also controls the body's automatic functions such as breathing, heartbeat, digestion, growth, and blood pressure.

QUICK FACTS

Our brains control our bodies by sending out billions of tiny electrical **SIGNALS** every second.

Even when asleep, the brain is just as **ACTIVE** as it is when awake, and sends nerve messages around itself.

The brain consumes about one-fifth of all the **ENERGY** used by the body.

Yet the brain forms only about **TWO PER CENT** of the whole body.

It uses 10 times as much energy for its **SIZE**, compared to other body parts.

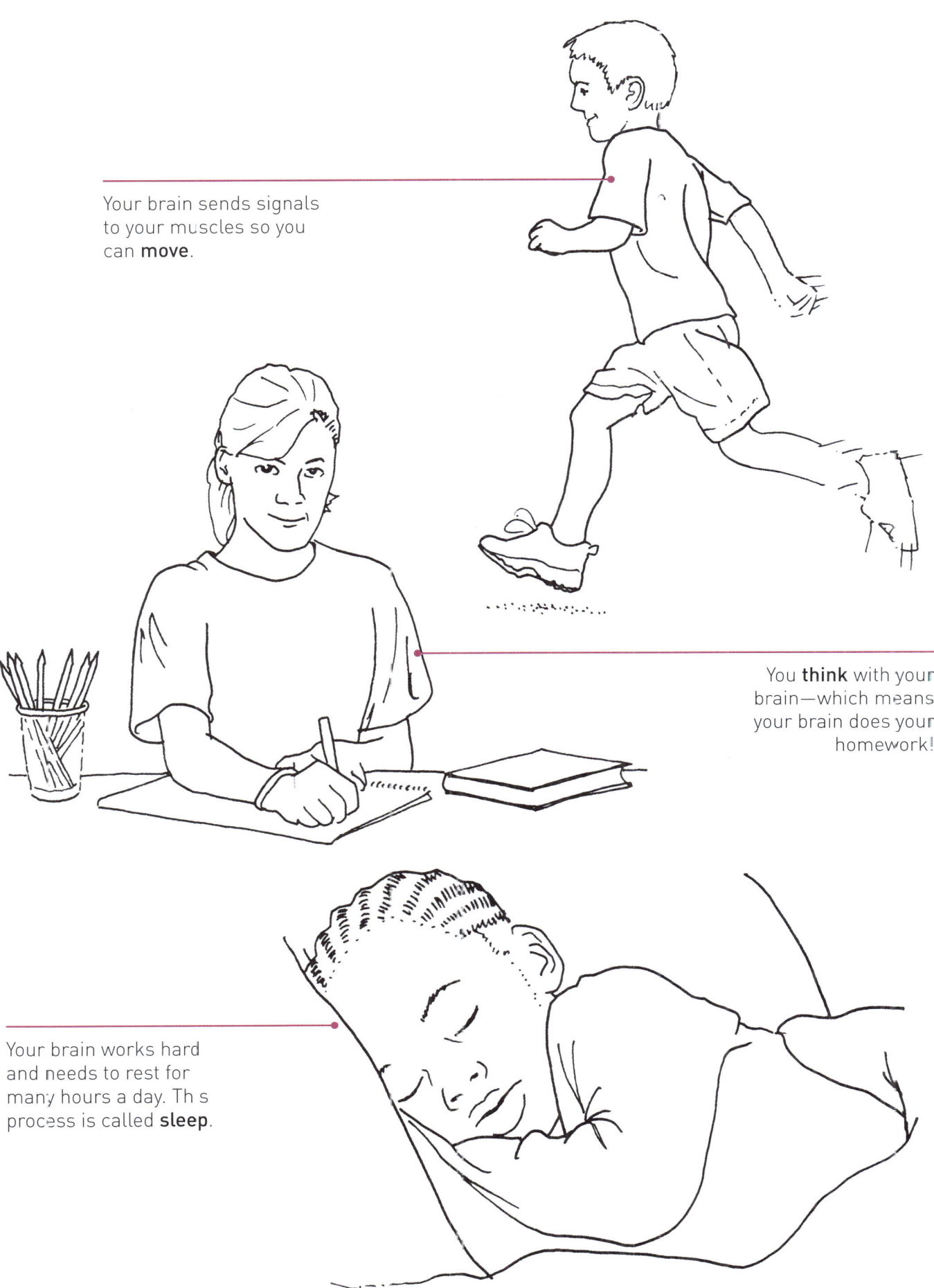

Your brain sends signals to your muscles so you can **move**.

You **think** with your brain—which means your brain does your homework!

Your brain works hard and needs to rest for many hours a day. This process is called **sleep**.

PARTS OF THE BRAIN

The brain is divided into three main regions, each with a different function. The basic functioning of your body, thinking and movement, are all very different processes, and need to be controlled and monitored in different ways.

QUICK FACTS

The cerebrum makes up more than **FOUR-FIFTHS** of the whole brain, and accounts for 85 per cent of its weight.

The **WEIGHT** of an average adult brain is 3.09 lbs.

The **LARGEST** accurately measured normal human brain weighs 6.4 lbs.

The brain is protected by the **CRANIUM**, the domed part of your skull.

The cerebrum is more **DEVELOPED** in humans than in any animals.

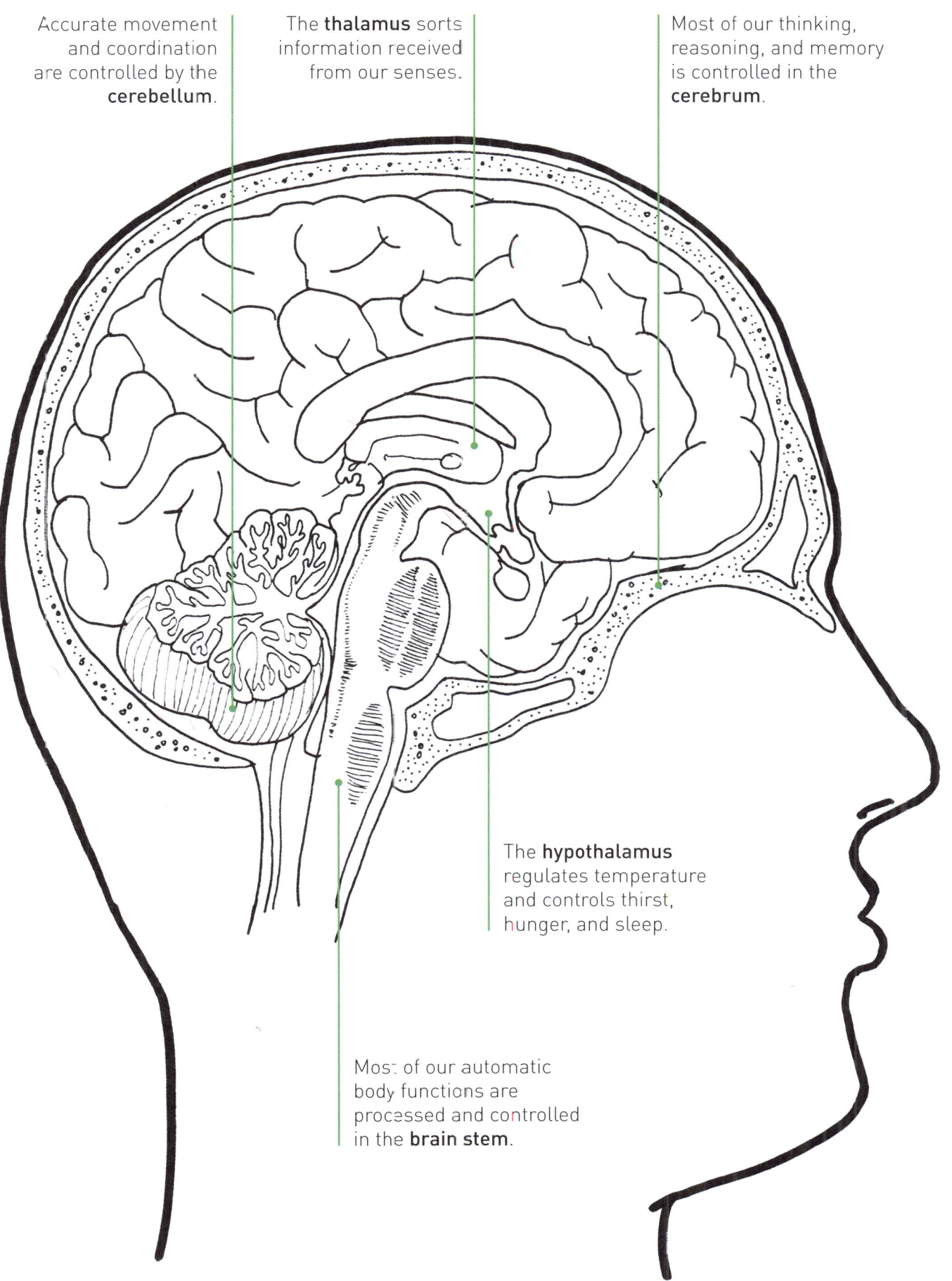

LEFT AND RIGHT BRAIN

Each side of the brain controls the opposite side of the body. Usually the left side controls speaking, writing, and logical thought, while the right controls artistic abilities.

In a right-handed person, the left side of the brain is dominant. In a left-handed person, the right side is dominant.

QUICK FACTS

A person may **WRITE** with one hand, but use the other to carry out everyday tasks.

About four per cent of the population is **LEFT-HANDED**.

In the course of history many of the greatest **GENIUSES** have also been left-handed.

Leonardo da Vinci and Michelangelo, the greatest **SCULPTORS** of all times, were both left-handed.

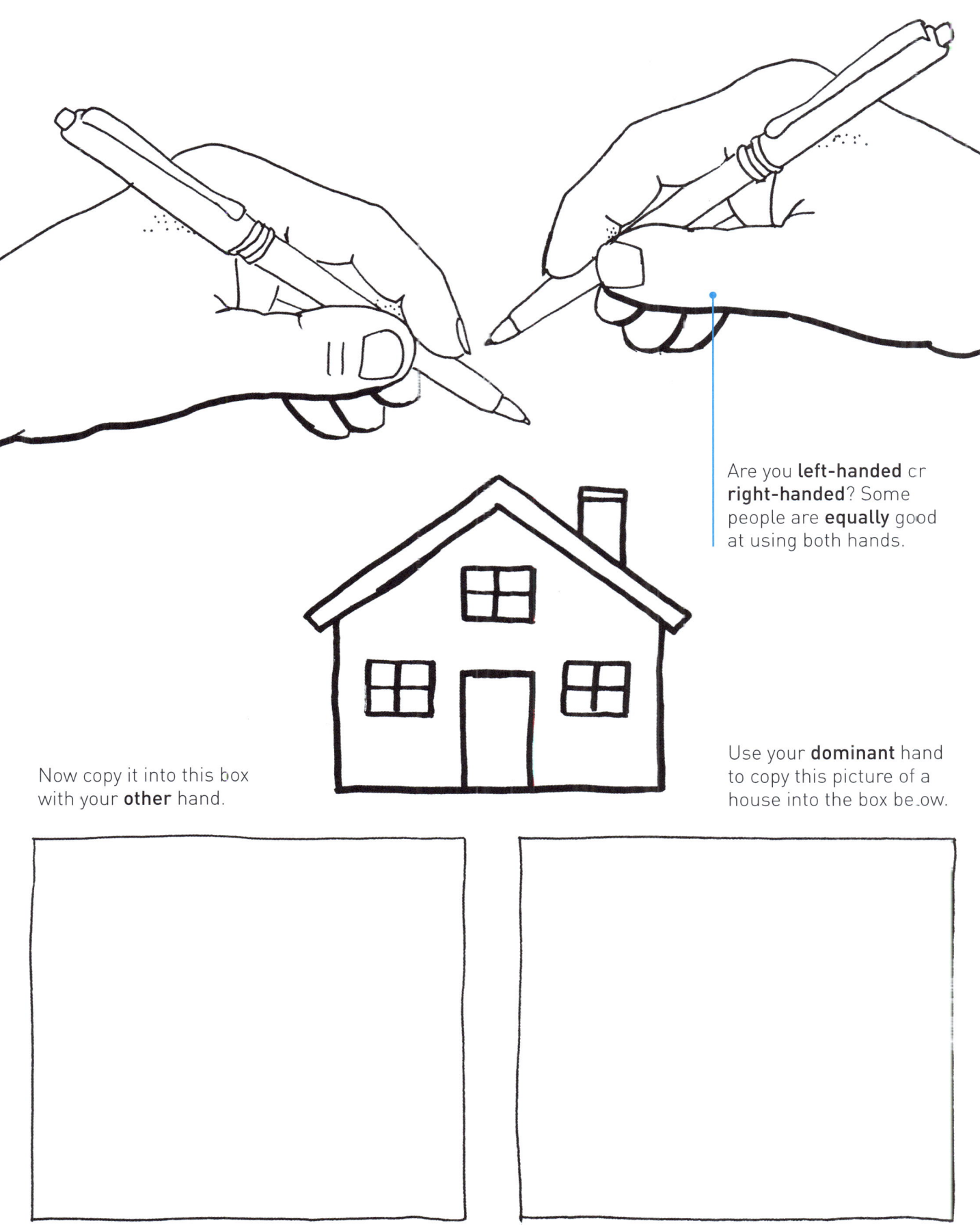

Are you **left-handed** or **right-handed**? Some people are **equally** good at using both hands.

Use your **dominant** hand to copy this picture of a house into the box below.

Now copy it into this box with your **other** hand.

CONTROL CENTER 17

NERVES

Messages are sent to the brain from different parts of the body and back through the nerves. A nerve impulse is like a very simple message: it's either on or off.

Because there are so many neurons (nerve paths) connected to one another, this simple signal is enough to carry the most complicated messages throughout the whole of the body's nervous system.

QUICK FACTS

A nerve **SIGNAL** is a tiny pulse of electricity, made by moving chemicals into and out of a nerve cell.

Nerves are bendy but **TOUGH**, so they can move easily at joints but withstand being squeezed by muscles.

There are nerves to **EVERY** body part, including the heart, lungs, and guts.

Individual nerve cells do not actually touch. The ends are separated by tiny gaps that are called **SYNAPSES**.

As a **nerve impulse** arrives at the junction between two nerve cells, it is carried across the gap or synapse by chemicals called neurotransmitters. These contact sensitive areas in the next nerve cell, and the nerve impulse is carried along.

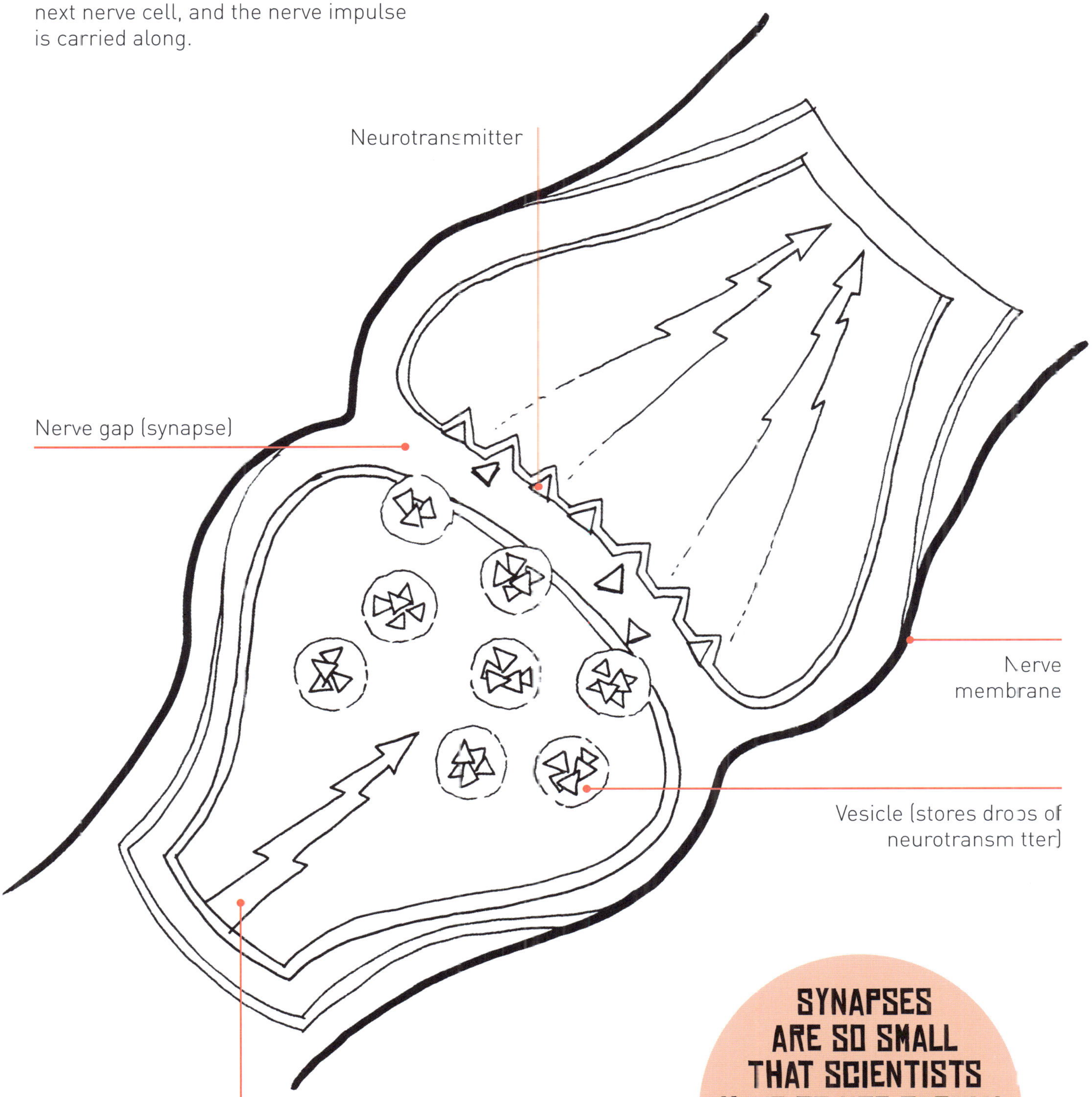

Neurotransmitter

Nerve gap (synapse)

Nerve membrane

Vesicle (stores drops of neurotransmitter)

Arriving nerve impulse

SYNAPSES ARE SO SMALL THAT SCIENTISTS HAVE TO USE SPECIAL ELECTRON MICROSCOPES TO STUDY THEM.

CONTROL CENTER 19

THE NERVOUS SYSTEM

We all have a nerve system to control our every movement and action, and every process that happens inside the body.

Your nervous system is made up of your brain, spinal cord, and nerves. It works by sending tiny electrical signals called nerve impulses. Millions of these travel around the body and brain every second, like the busiest computer network.

QUICK FACTS

Nerve **IMPULSES** travel along the largest nerve fibers at 295 ft per second!

When you hurt a finger you probably feel the touch first, and then the pain starts a moment later. This is because the signals for touch travel **FASTER** along the nerves than the signals for pain.

All the nerves in the body, taken out and joined end to end, would stretch about **62 MILES**.

The longest single nerve **FIBERS**, in the legs, are up to a yard in length.

The **THICKEST** nerve in the human body is the sciatic nerve, located in the hip and thigh. It is about the width of its owner's thumb.

The **SPINAL CORD** is usually the width of its owner's little finger.

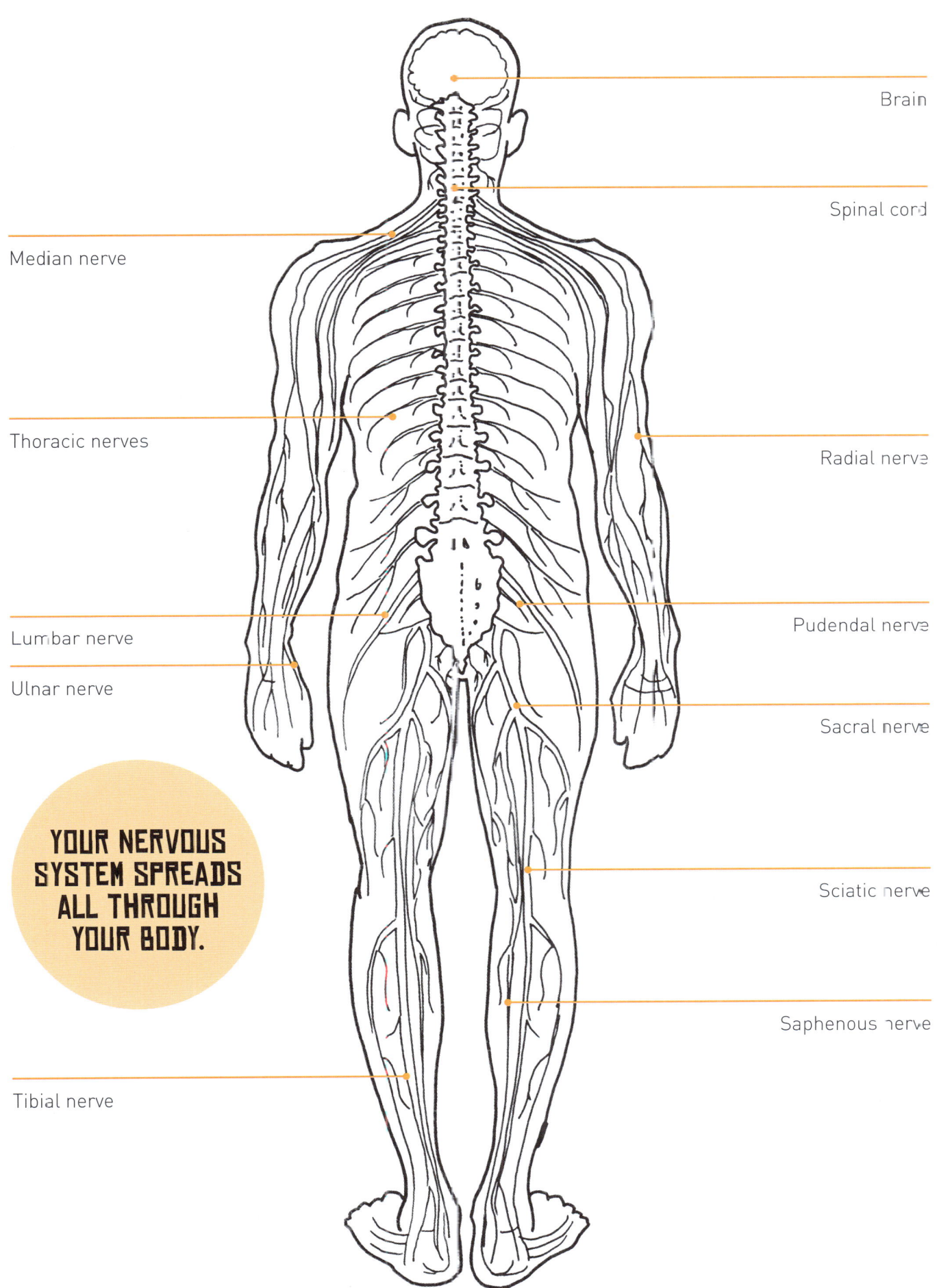

HEART AND LUNGS

WHAT IS BLOOD?

Blood carries useful substances such as oxygen and nutrients to all the body parts. Pumped by the heart, it flows through tubes called blood vessels.

It also collects waste and unwanted substances, and these are removed mainly by the kidneys. However, apart from this delivery and collection service, blood does much, much more.

QUICK FACTS

Blood is **WARM** and works like the liquid in a central heating system. It absorbs warmth from the busy parts such as the heart and muscles, and spreads it out to cooler parts like the skin.

Just over half of blood is **PLASMA**, a pale yellow, sweet-smelling, sticky fluid.

Over nine-tenths of blood is **WATER**.

Blood contains disease-fighting **ANTIBODIES**. It helps seal cuts and wounds, by clotting.

Your blood makes up about eight per cent of your body **WEIGHT**.

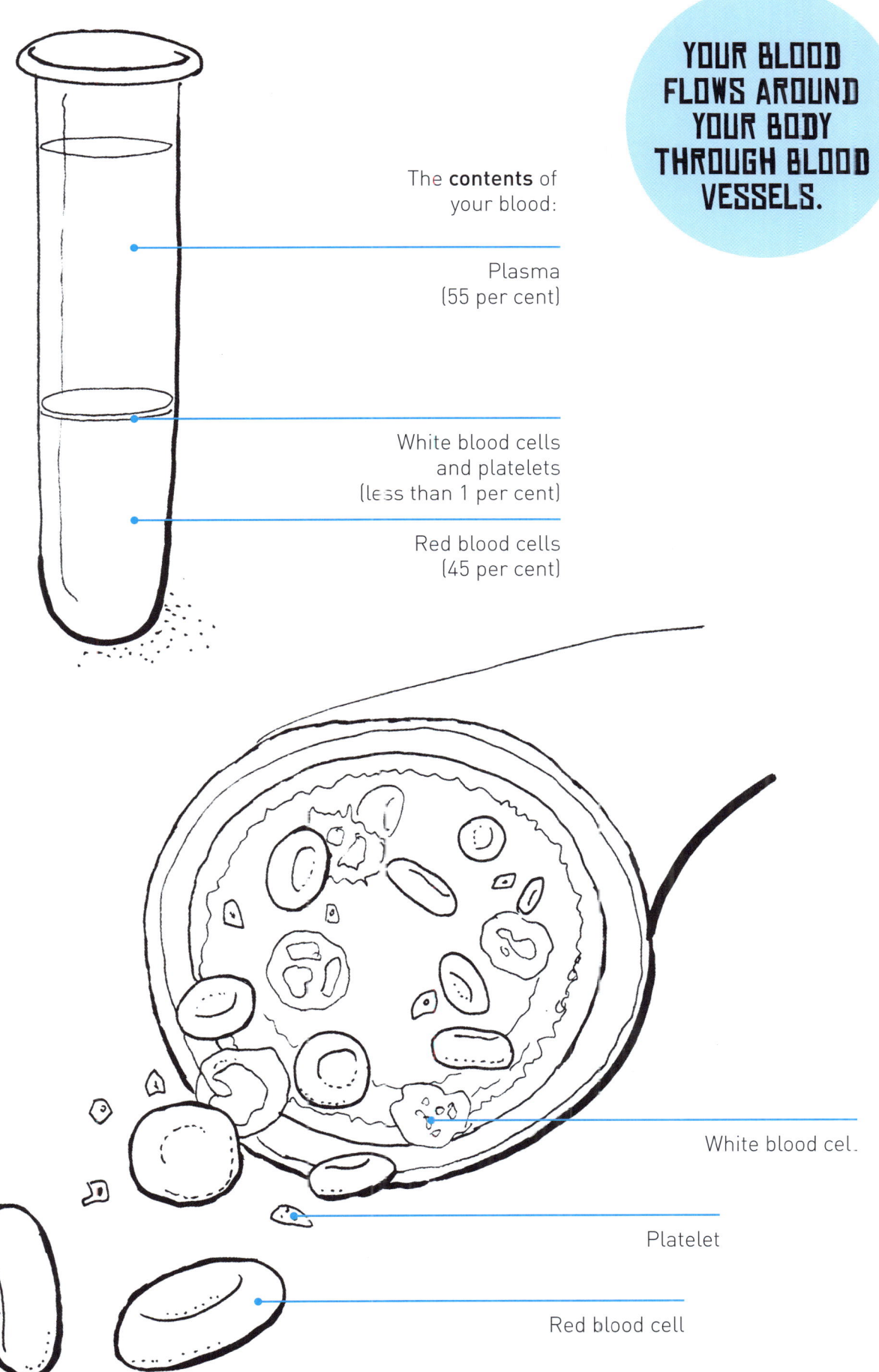

The **contents** of your blood:

Plasma (55 per cent)

White blood cells and platelets (less than 1 per cent)

Red blood cells (45 per cent)

YOUR BLOOD FLOWS AROUND YOUR BODY THROUGH BLOOD VESSELS.

White blood cell

Platelet

Red blood cell

HEART AND LUNGS

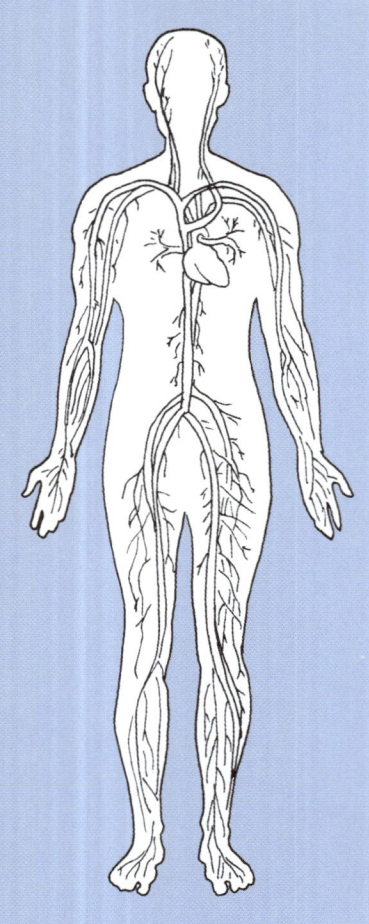

THE HEART

In the center of your chest, below a thin layer of skin, muscle, and bone, sits your heart. This simple, yet essential, pump carries blood to and from your body's billions of cells, non-stop, day and night.

The heart is between the lungs. It tips slightly to the left side, which is why people think it is on the left side of the body.

QUICK FACTS

Without the heart's second-by-second **COLLECTION** and **DELIVERY** service, your cells—and your body—would die.

The heart is about the size of its owner's clenched **FIST**. As you grow from a child into an adult, your heart grows at the same rate as your fist.

The heart contains the **AORTA**, the largest artery in the body. It is about the diameter of a garden hose.

An adult has an average resting **HEART RATE** of about 75 beats per minute.

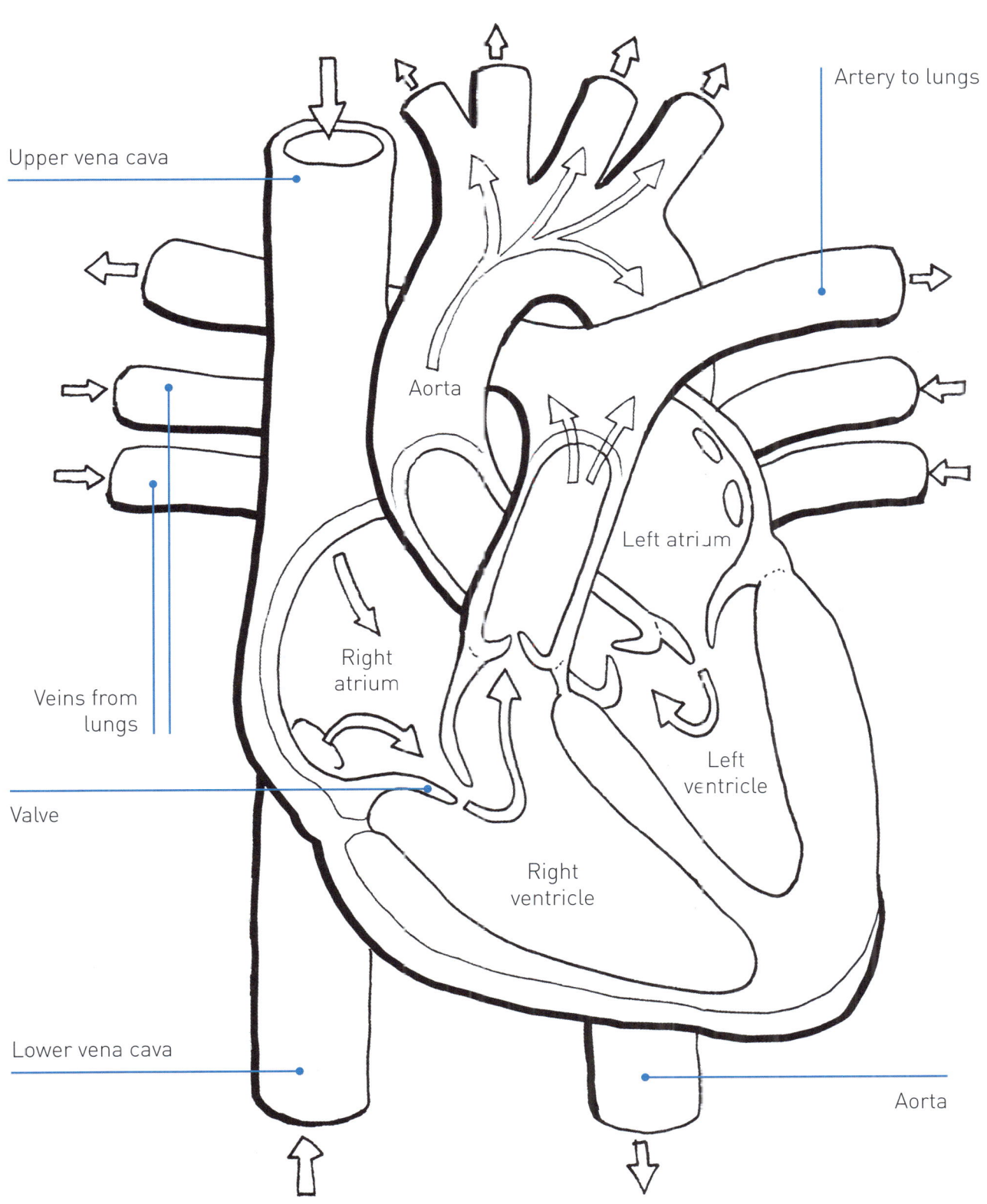

VEINS AND ARTERIES

Blood is pumped around your body in a continuous flow from the heart. It travels inside a network of tubes called blood vessels—arteries, veins, and capillaries.

The blood in arteries comes straight from the heart and is pumped under pressure, so the artery walls are thick and muscular. Veins return blood to the heart, and because the pressure is lower, they have thinner walls than arteries.

QUICK FACTS

Veins look **BLUE** because of a trick of the light. In reality, this blood is a very dark red.

The blood in your veins travels quite slowly, and many large veins have **VALVES** to stop the blood from draining backward toward your legs and feet.

In general, arteries lie **DEEP** within the body, and veins nearer the **SURFACE**.

"Going for the **JUGULAR**" means attacking someone at their weakest point. It refers to the vulnerability of the jugular vein, which is in your neck.

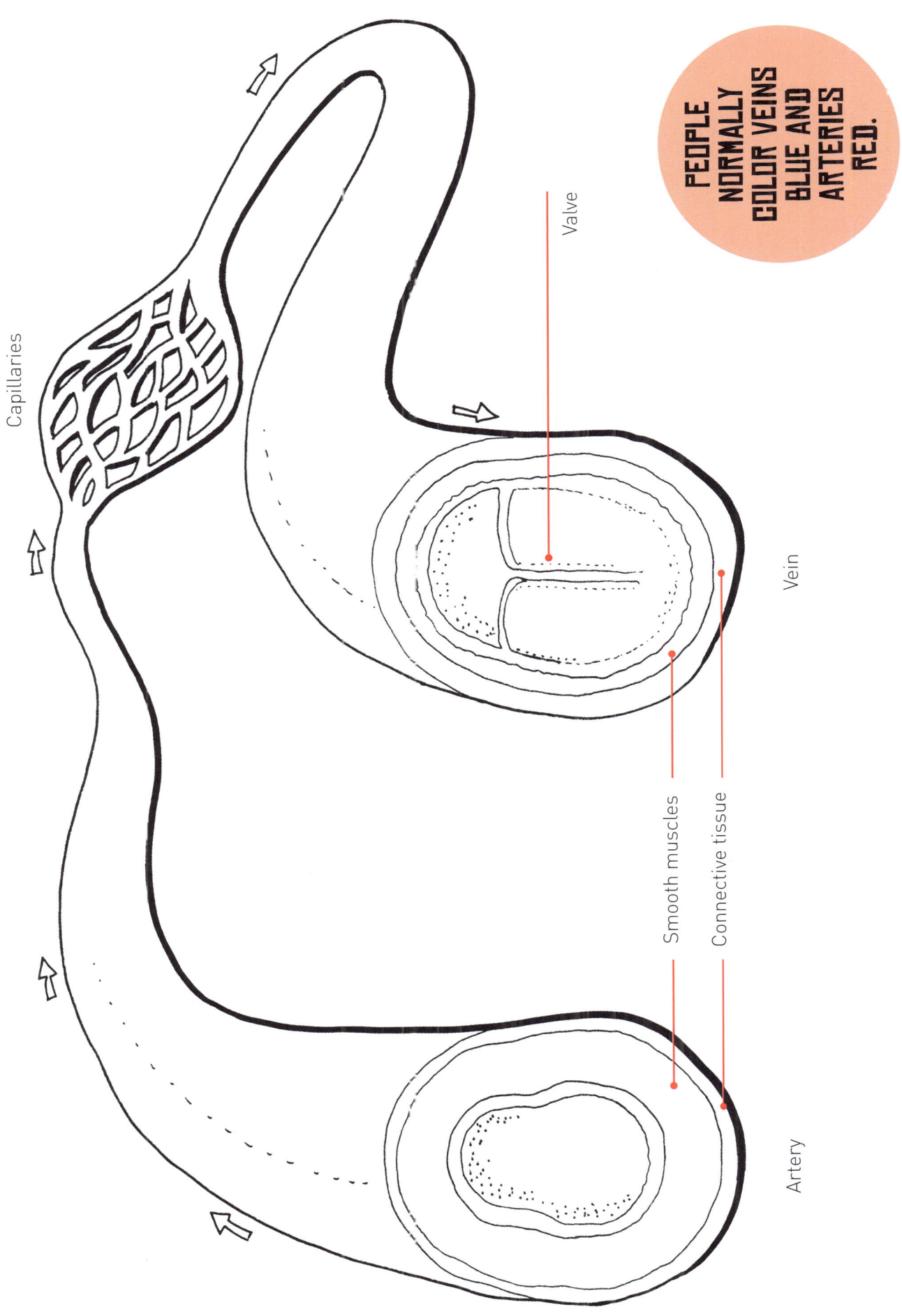

HEART AND LUNGS 29

CAPILLARIES

Blood moves from arteries to veins through tiny capillaries. The capillaries also allow excess fluid to escape from the blood.

They are too small to be seen without a microscope, and so narrow that red blood cells have to squash themselves up to pass through.

QUICK FACTS

The cells in blood flow through a capillary for only **HALF A SECOND** before they move on into small veins.

Laid out end to end, an adult's veins, arteries, and capillaries would be about **60,000 MILES** long!

About one-sixth of all the body's **BLOOD** is in the arteries, almost three-quarters is in the veins, and less than one-twentieth is in the tiny capillaries inside the organs.

If all your capillaries were ironed flat, they would cover a **SOCCER PITCH**.

WHY DO WE BREATHE?

Breathing is when you draw air in through your nose and mouth, and into your lungs. Like all your movements, it relies on muscle power.

We breathe in order to get oxygen from the air. Oxygen is the gas our bodies use to convert nutrients into energy. We breathe out to get rid of carbon dioxide, a waste gas that our bodies cannot use.

QUICK FACTS

INHALED air contains 20 per cent oxygen, 0.03 per cent carbon dioxide, and the rest is nitrogen.

EXHALED air contains 16 per cent oxygen, and the carbon dioxide is increased by more than a hundred times to four per cent.

The average person at **REST** breathes in and out about 10–14 times per minute.

If you sing or play an **INSTRUMENT** like a trumpet, you need lots of puff. Learn to use the muscle under your lungs to get more lung power.

We breathe **heavily** after exercise, in order to take in more oxygen.

WE BREATHE IN DIFFERENT WAYS AT DIFFERENT TIMES.

We breathe **smoothly** and **deeply** when we are concentrating, for example while doing homework.

Sometimes breathing while asleep makes you **snore**! There are several different causes for snoring.

HEART AND LUNGS

HOW DO WE BREATHE?

When we breathe, air enters through the nose or mouth and travels down the windpipe. The windpipe forks into other tubes called bronchi, which lead into the lungs.

Breathe in deeply and watch your ribs rise and your chest expand. Your muscles make your chest bigger and stretch the spongy lungs inside.

QUICK FACTS

You breathe every few **SECONDS** throughout your life, even when you are asleep.

The right lung is often a little **LARGER** than the left.

Underwater animals, like fish, have breathing organs called **GILLS** instead of lungs. These can take in oxygen from the water.

To enable us to breathe underwater, humans need an **OXYGEN TANK**, because if our lungs filled with water we would drown.

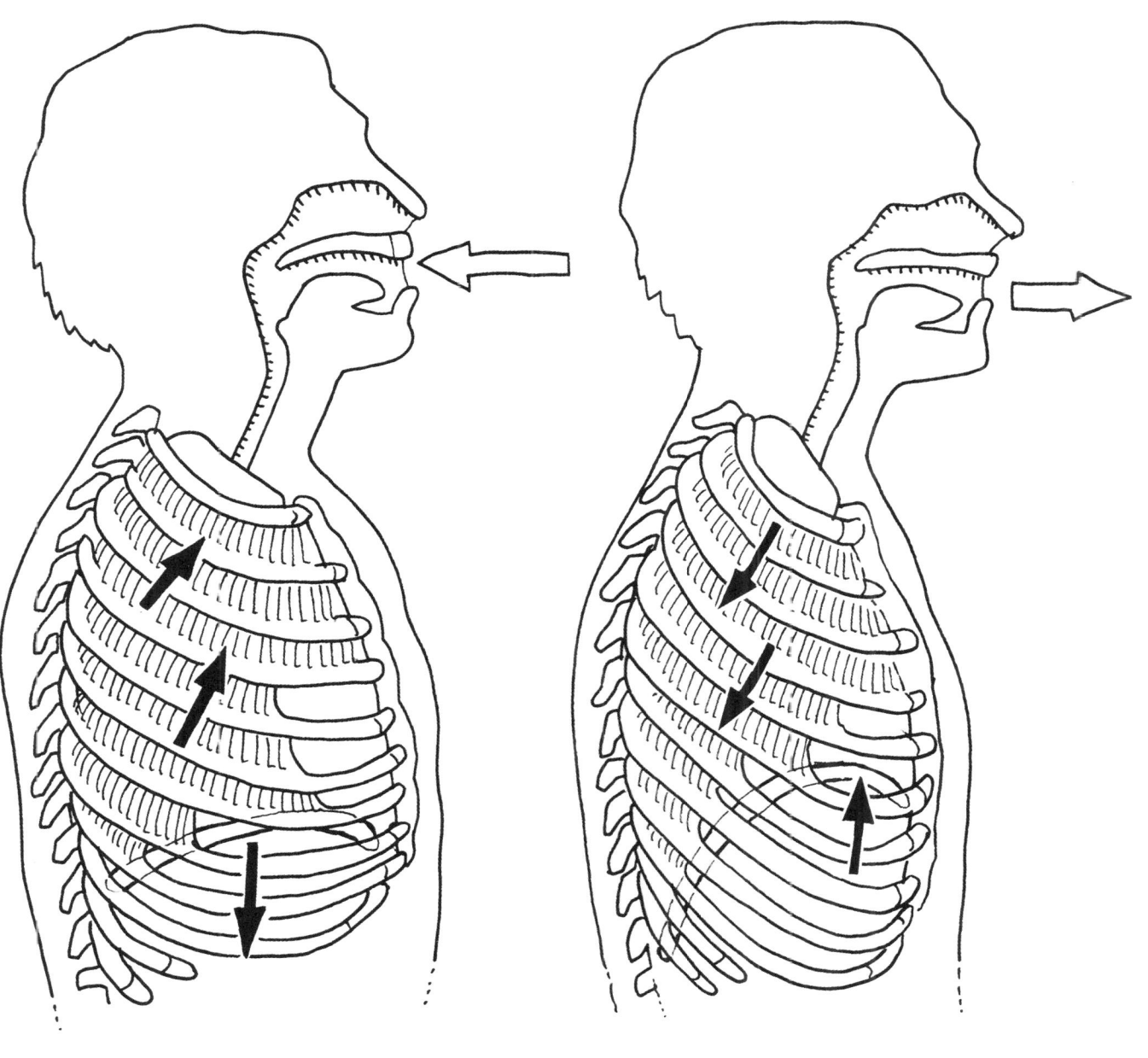

Breathing in
Your ribcage is **pushed out**

Your diaphragm is **pushed down**

Your lungs **expand**

Air **enters** the oral cavity (mouth)

Breathing out
Your ribcage is **pulled in**

Your diaphragm **rises**

Your lungs **contract**

Air **exits** the oral cavity (mouth)

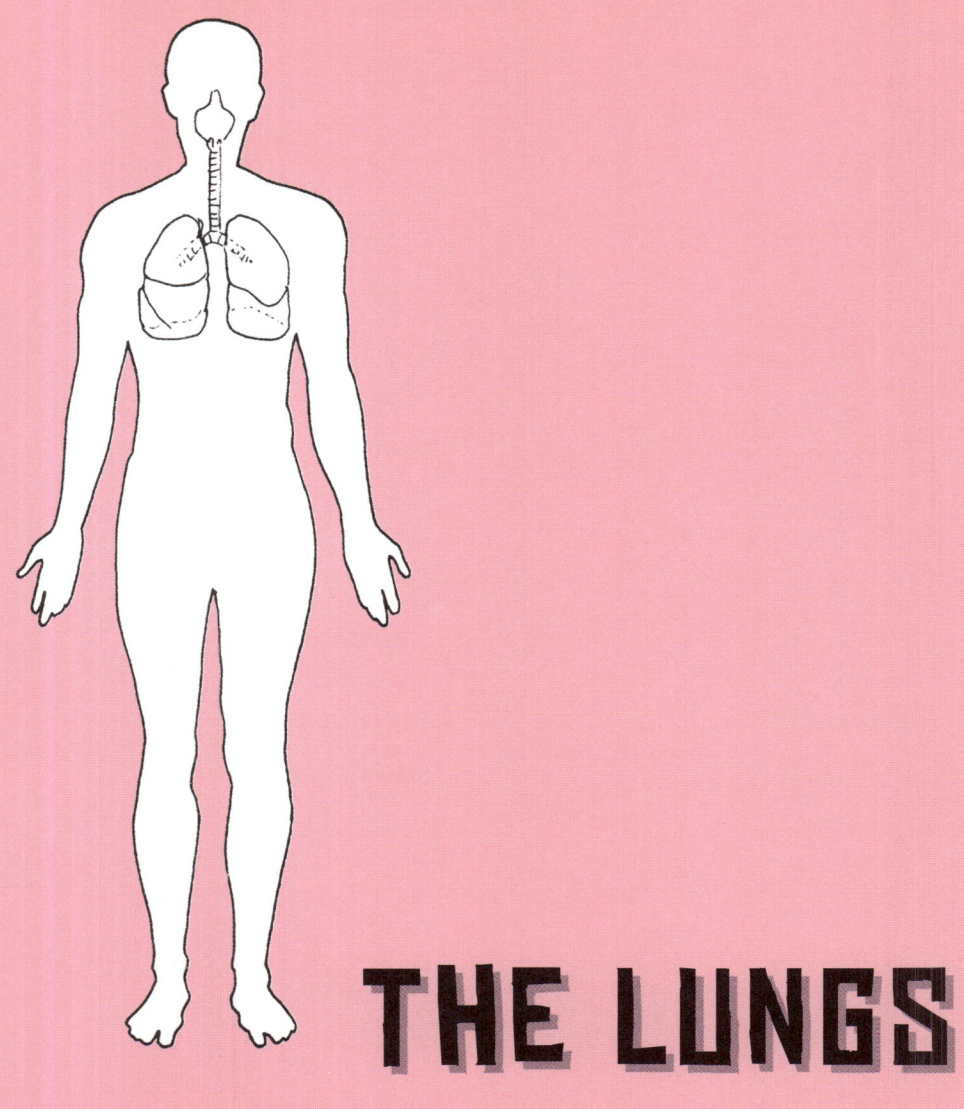

THE LUNGS

You have two lungs, one in each side of your chest, enclosed by an airtight box.

When you breathe in and out, your lungs go up and down rather like balloons, but they aren't just hollow bags. They are spongy organs made up of tightly packed tissue, nerves, and blood vessels.

QUICK FACTS

The whole breathing apparatus is designed to bring fresh **AIR** as close as possible to the blood.

The left lung has two main parts, or **LOBES**, and a scooped-out shape where the heart fits.

The right lung has three lobes and is on average about one-fifth **BIGGER** than the left lung.

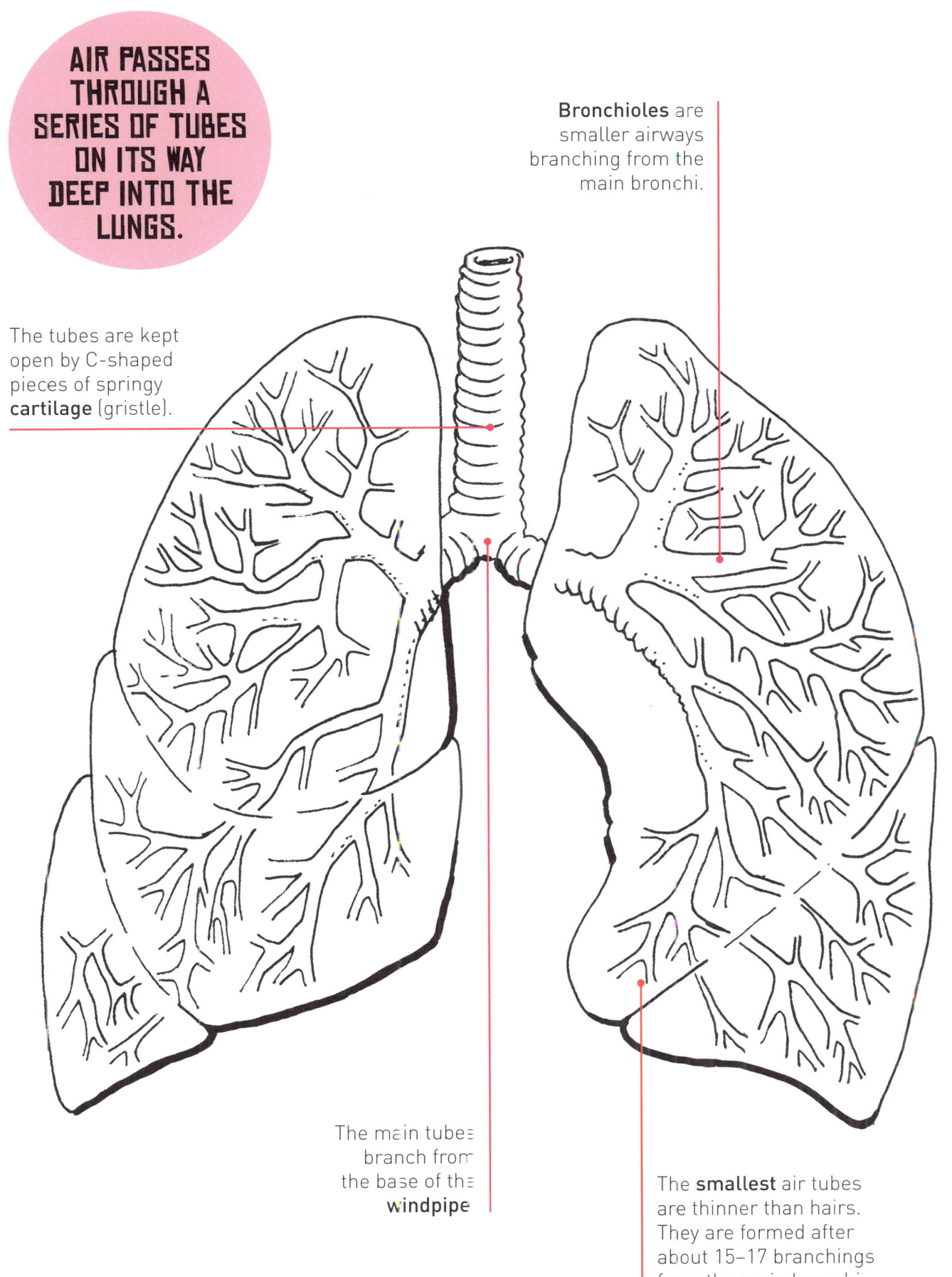

AIR PASSES THROUGH A SERIES OF TUBES ON ITS WAY DEEP INTO THE LUNGS.

Bronchioles are smaller airways branching from the main bronchi.

The tubes are kept open by C-shaped pieces of springy **cartilage** (gristle).

The main tubes branch from the base of the **windpipe**.

The **smallest** air tubes are thinner than hairs. They are formed after about 15–17 branchings from the main bronchi.

HEART AND LUNGS 37

INSIDE THE LUNGS

The places where oxygen is taken into the body are tiny bubble-shaped spaces deep in the lungs called alveoli. Alveoli are bunched at the end of the smallest airways, the bronchioles.

The walls of the alveoli are so thin that oxygen and carbon dioxide can pass through them.

QUICK FACTS

There are 250–300 million alveoli in each **LUNG**.

If the **WALLS** of the alveoli could be spread out flat, they would cover about half a tennis court!

Alveoli are delicate, and can be damaged by many different things, thus causing us to **COUGH**.

Each alveolar **DUCT** in the lungs supplies about 20 alveoli.

The very thin walls of each alveolus contain networks of extremely small blood vessels called **CAPILLARIES**.

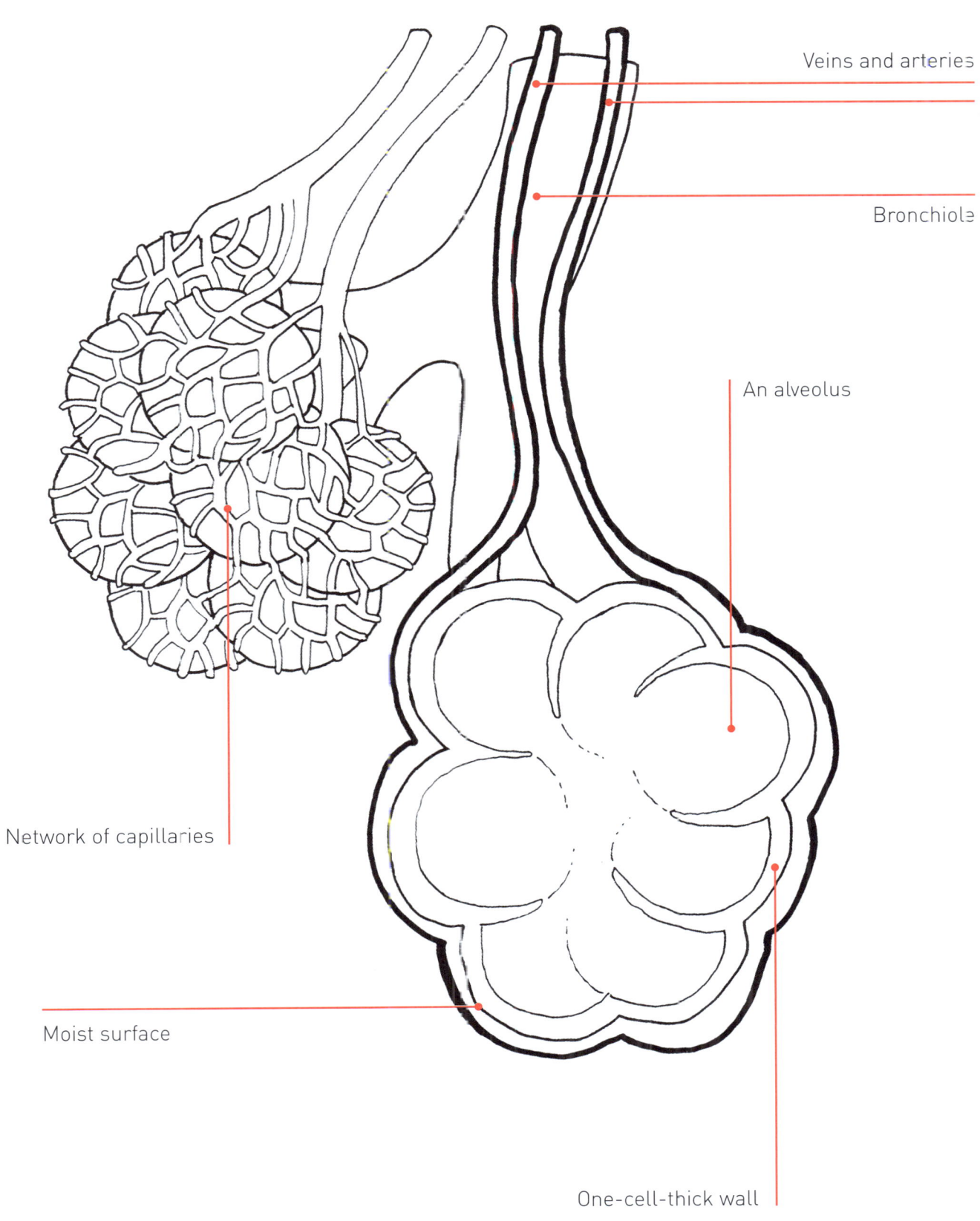

EATING AND DIGESTION

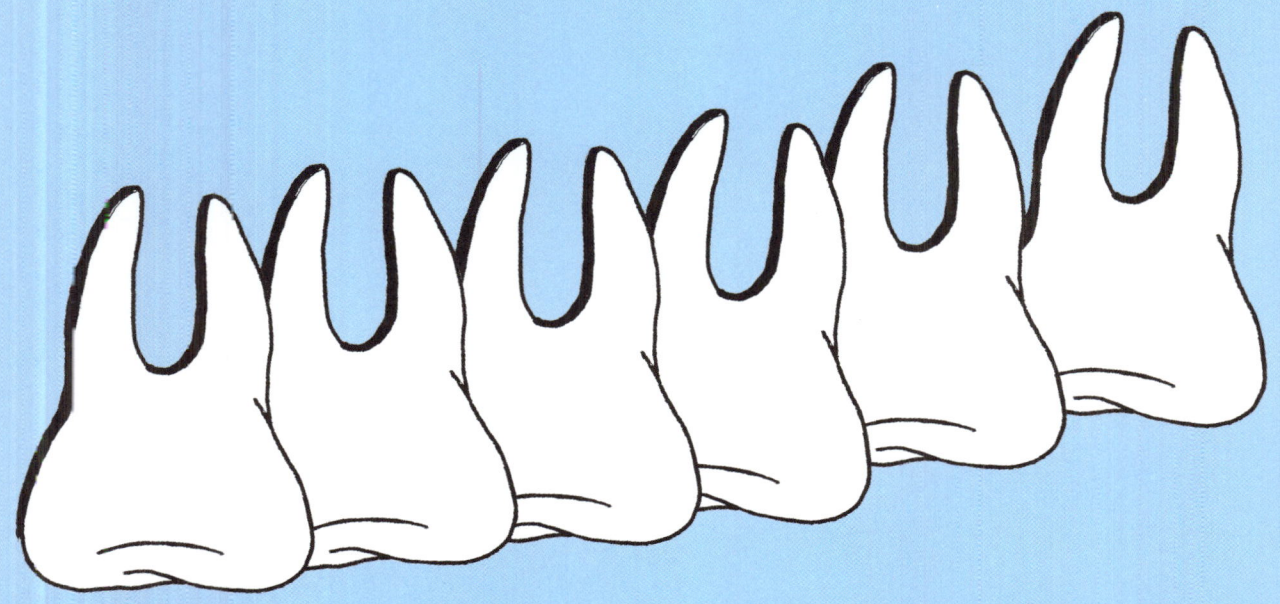

TEETH

Humans have four kinds of teeth: incisors, canines, premolars, and molars. They are differently shaped, so they can carry out different jobs.

QUICK FACTS

Your back teeth are **BUMPY** on top. They work together, grinding food between the bumps.

No two sets of teeth are the same. Your teeth are as **UNIQUE** as your fingerprints.

As the **SURFACE** of a tooth wears away, the tooth grows farther out of its socket, exposing the root.

WISDOM teeth are a mystery. Nobody has discovered exactly why we have them, and what their purpose is!

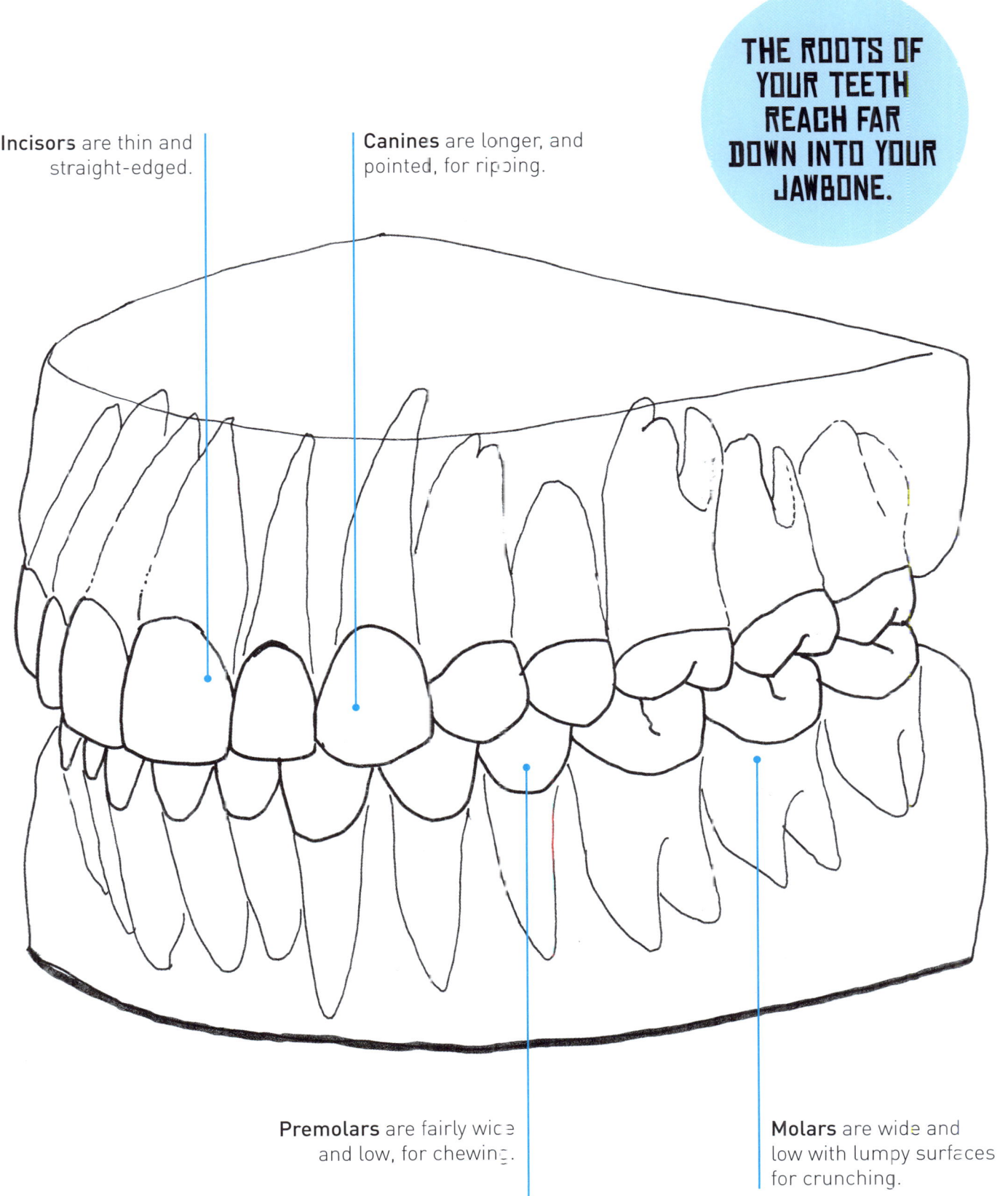

Incisors are thin and straight-edged.

Canines are longer, and pointed, for ripping.

THE ROOTS OF YOUR TEETH REACH FAR DOWN INTO YOUR JAWBONE.

Premolars are fairly wide and low, for chewing.

Molars are wide and low with lumpy surfaces for crunching.

EATING AND DIGESTION 43

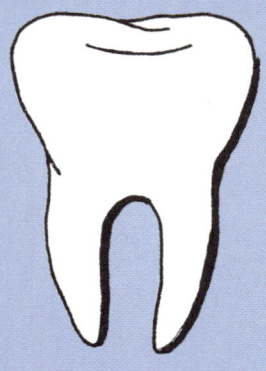

INSIDE A TOOTH

Each tooth has two main parts. The root anchors it firmly in the gum, to withstand the tremendous pressures that are exerted when you bite and chew hard foods like nuts. The crown is the visible part above the gum. It is covered with whitish enamel, which is the hardest substance in the entire body.

QUICK FACTS

PULP is the innermost layer of a tooth. It consists of connective tissue, blood vessels, and nerves.

DENTINE is harder than bone, and takes up most of a tooth. It consists mainly of mineral salts and water, but also has some living cells.

ENAMEL is the hardest tissue in the body. It enables a tooth to withstand the pressure placed on it during chewing.

CEMENTUM overlays the dentine in the root of the tooth. In most cases, the cementum and enamel meet where the root ends and the crown begins.

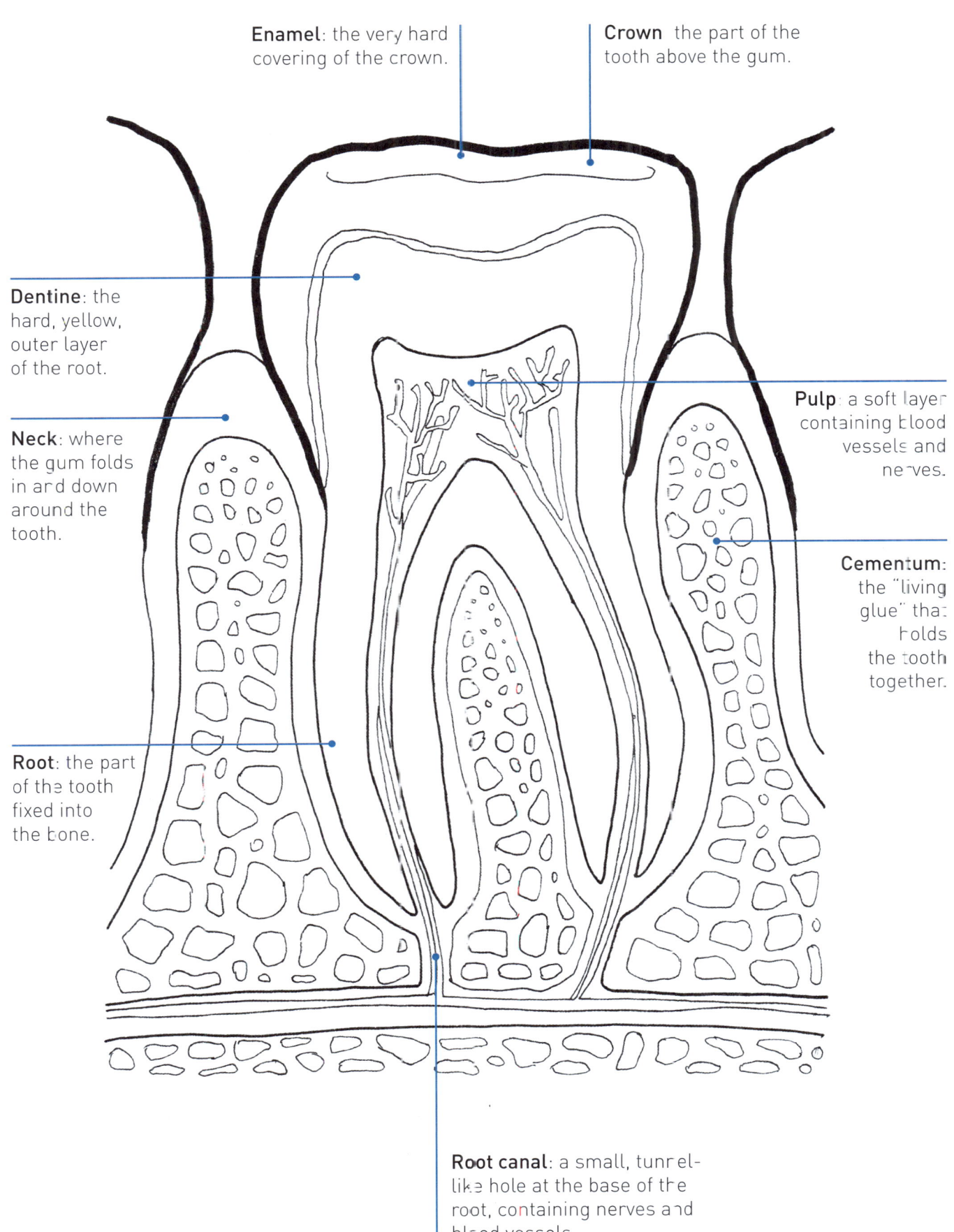

DIGESTION

A car needs gasoline (petrol), a truck uses diesel, and a jet plane runs on kerosene. These are all fuels that provide the energy needed to make machines go. Your "body machine" needs fuel too, and it gets it in the form of food.

Digestion is the process of changing the food we eat so that it can be used by the body.

QUICK FACTS

The parts of the body specialized for taking in and breaking down foods into tiny pieces are called the **DIGESTIVE SYSTEM**.

The contents of your stomach are **CHURNED** about to mix the digestive juices throughout the food.

The digestive system makes more than 2.6 gallons of digestive **JUICES** each day.

Most of the **WATER** in these juices is taken back into the body by the large intestine.

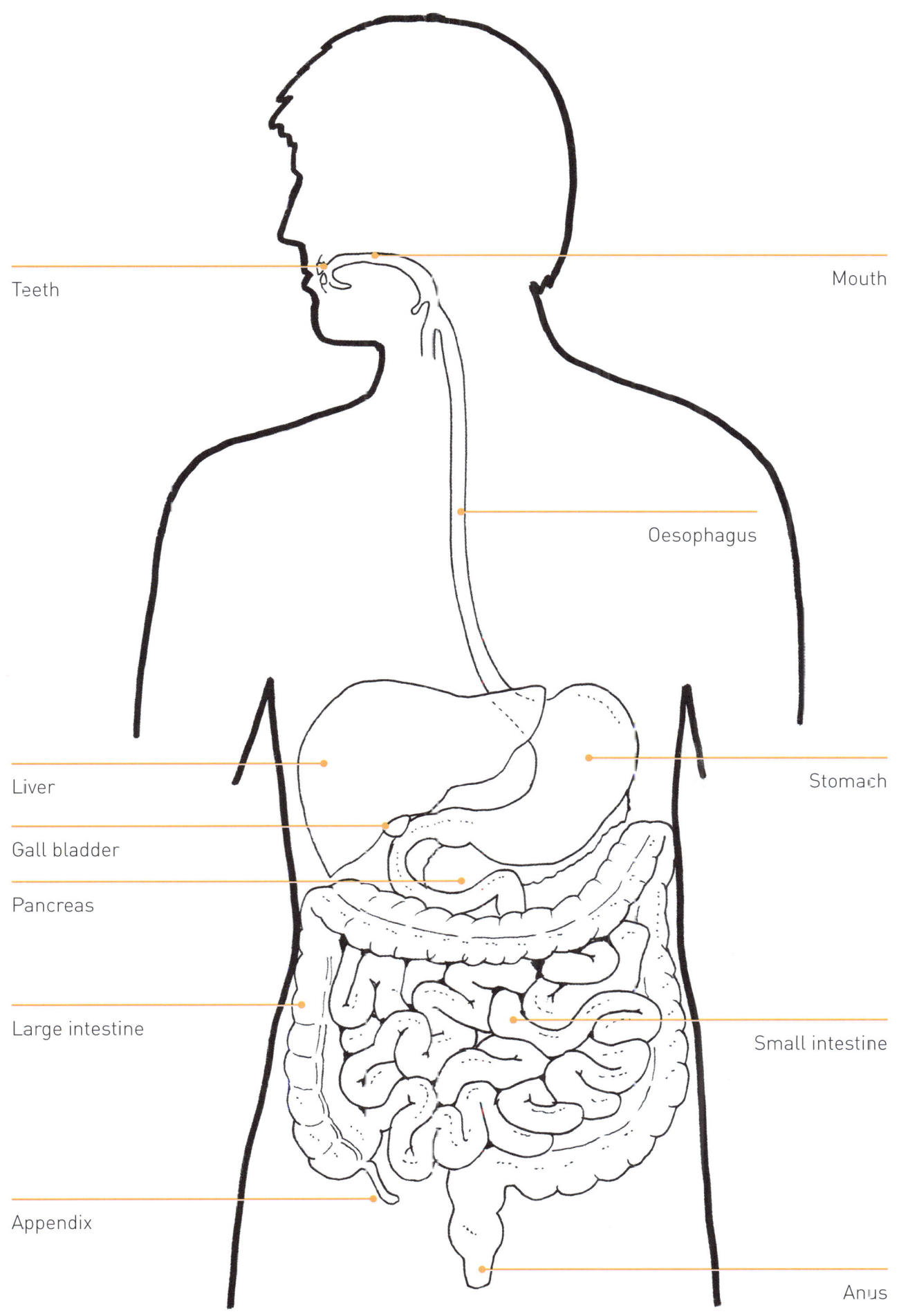

THE MOUTH

Digestion begins with the first bite. In your mouth the food is chopped up and chewed by your teeth and mixed with saliva.

Your tongue moistens and crushes your food and kneads it into a ball. This ball of food is then pushed down a short tube called the oesophagus to your stomach.

QUICK FACTS

The mouth is also known as the **ORAL CAVITY**.

Everyone's mouth is full of **BACTERIA**, although not all bacteria are harmful.

The **ROOF** of the mouth has two main parts. The front part behind the nose is called the hard palate, and the rear part above the back of the mouth is the soft palate.

The palate can **BEND UP** as a lump of food is pushed to the back of the mouth by swallowing.

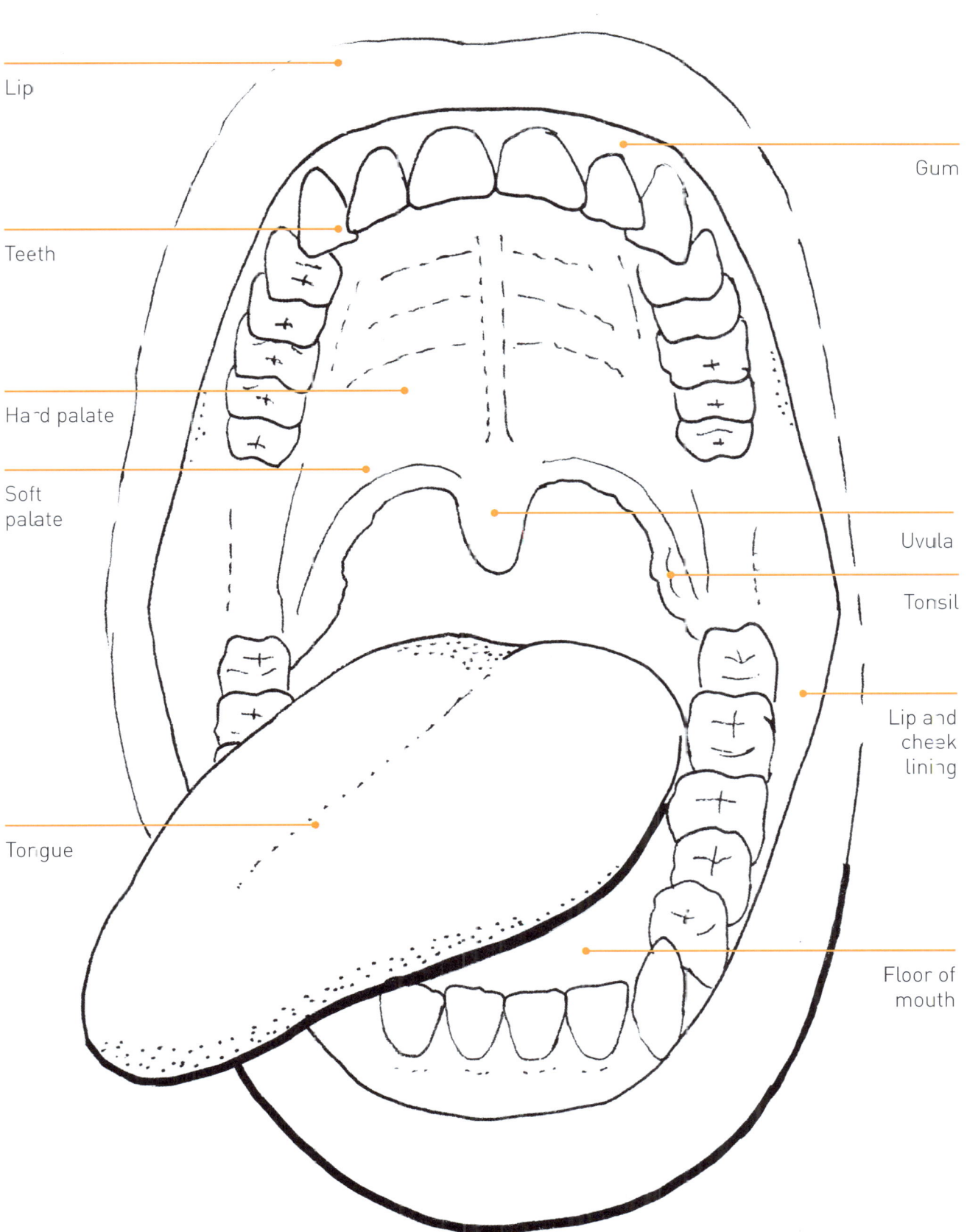

EATING AND DIGESTION 49

THE THROAT

The "throat" is a term loosely applied to the part of the neck in front of the backbone. It contains structures important in breathing and eating.

As you swallow, your windpipe is closed by your epiglottis. This forces the food into its own passage, the oesophagus.

QUICK FACTS

Without the epiglottis, food would go into your windpipe, and you would **CHOKE**.

Your epiglottis is a leaf-shaped **FLAP** above your voice box.

Muscular **WAVES** carry food down your oesophagus to your stomach.

Many of the muscles you use for **TALKING** are also used for swallowing.

As you swallow

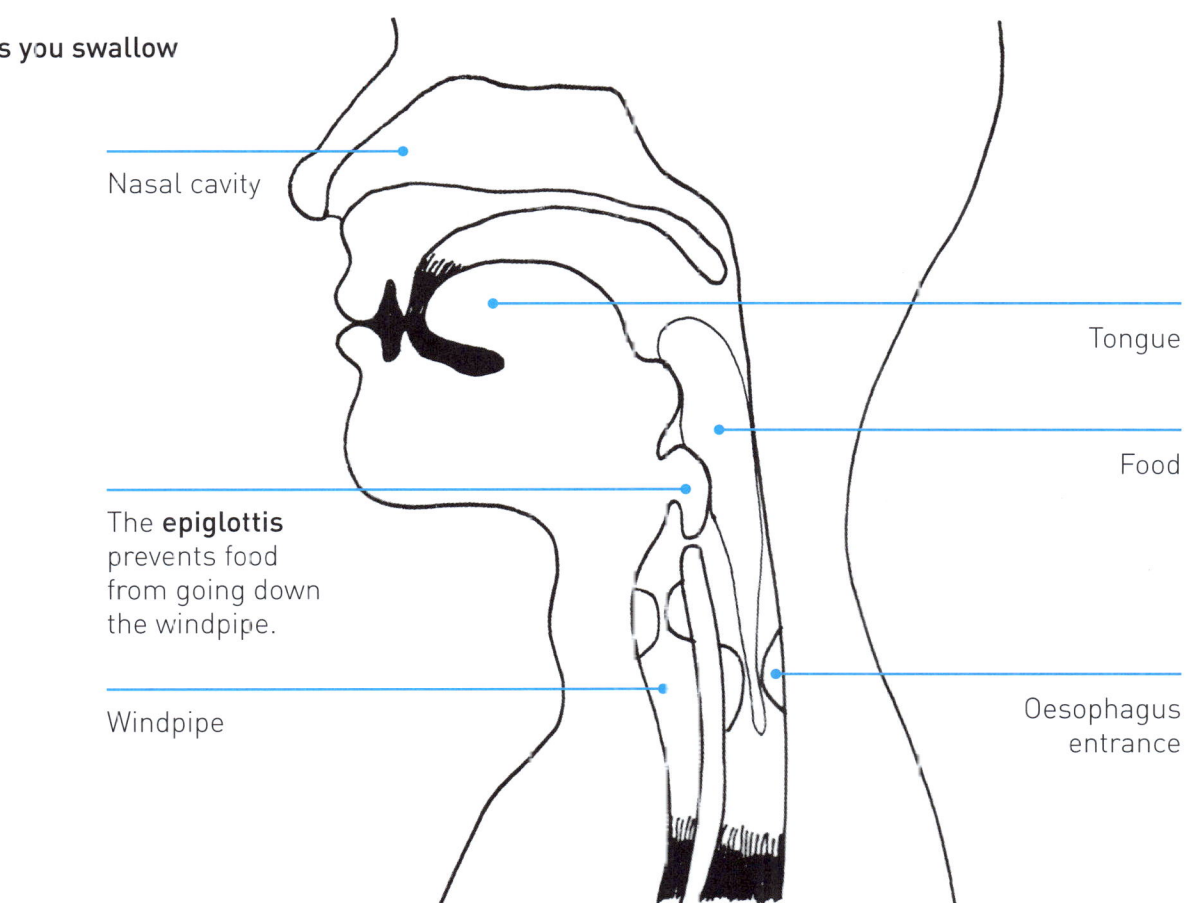

After the food has gone down

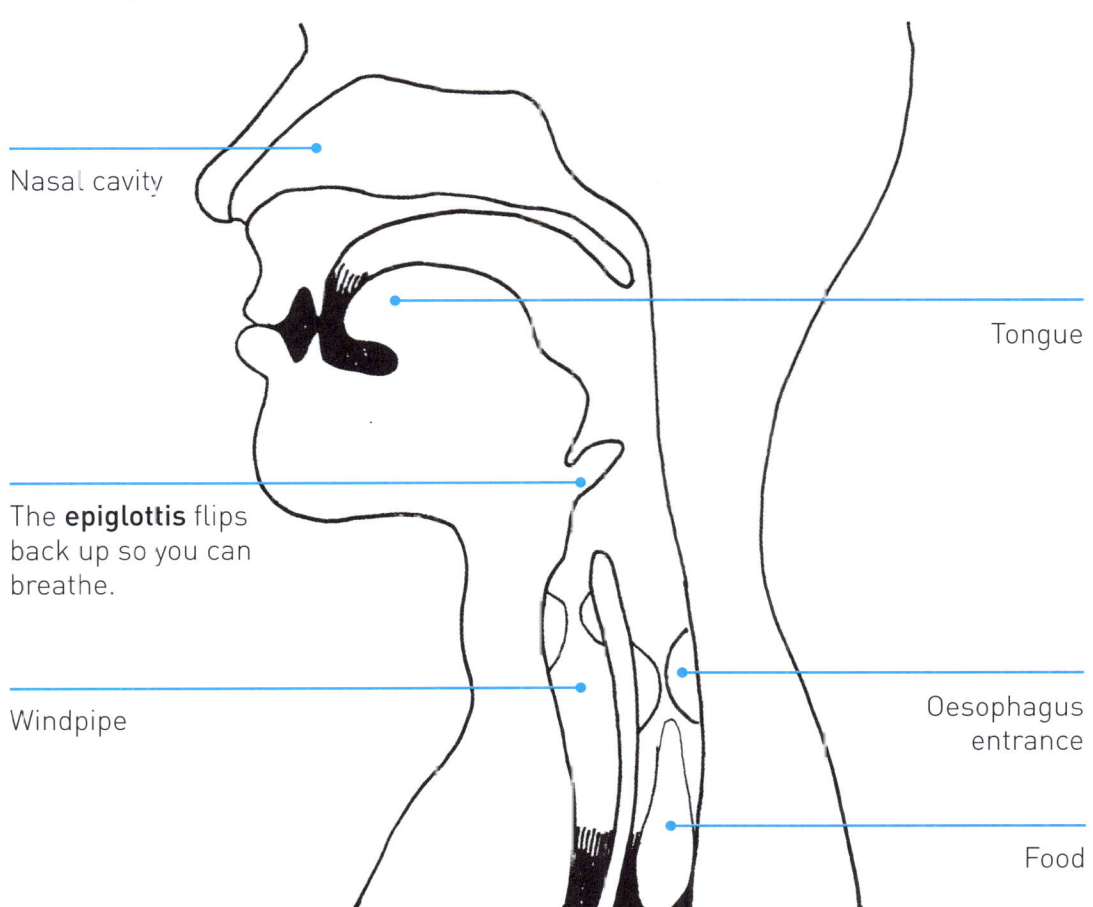

EATING AND DIGESTION 51

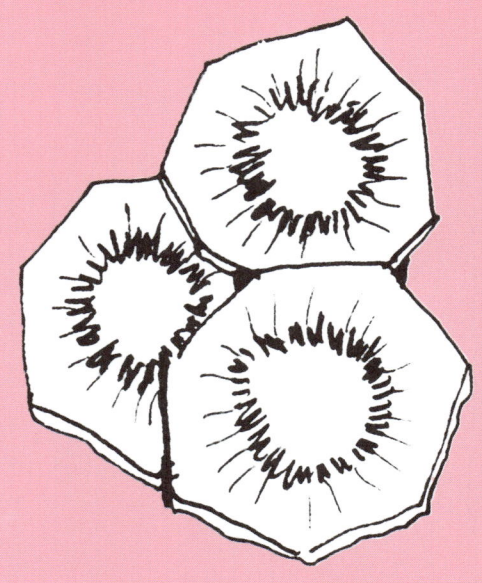

FOOD

We use one simple name for all the substances your body needs to take in: food.

However, in your food there are six main groups of material. They are: proteins, carbohydrates, fats, vitamins, minerals, and fiber.

QUICK FACTS

FATS are used for both building and energy.

CARBOHYDRATES are known as "energy foods".

FIBER is needed to help food to pass properly through the body.

PROTEINS provide some energy, but more importantly they serve as the main building materials of the body.

VITAMINS and **MINERALS** are a small but important part of your diet. There are many of them, and they each perform different roles.

Fruits and vegetables contain a lot of **fiber**, **vitamins**, and **minerals**.

Bread, rice, potatoes, and pasta are good sources of **carbohydrate**.

Meat and fish have lots of **protein**.

Fatty foods contain a lot of—you guessed it, **fat**!

Milk and dairy foods have many **minerals** and **protein**, but also sometimes a high level of **fat**.

EATING AND DIGESTION 53

VITAMINS

We need chemicals known as vitamins in order to stay alive. They are named by giving them letters, such as vitamin A, vitamin B, and so on.

If you lack certain vitamins, you will get ill. For example, without enough vitamin C, your blood vessels become fragile and bleed easily. Black and blue marks appear on the skin and near the eyes.

Vitamin C can be found in citrus fruits and fresh vegetables.

QUICK FACTS

FRUITS contain a wide range of essential vitamins and minerals.

Some vitamins are **STORED** in the body, while others need to be eaten every day.

In the past, sailors who went on long trips and couldn't get **FRESH** vegetables would develop a disease called scurvy. In the 17th century, British sailors were given lemons and limes to prevent this disease.

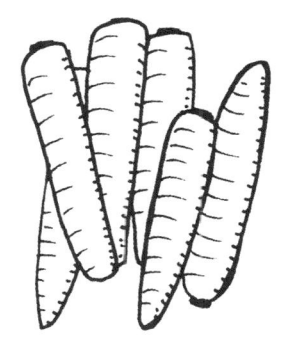

Carrots contain vitamin **A**.

Almonds contain vitamin **E**.

Spinach contains vitamin **K**.

Beans contain vitamin **B1**.

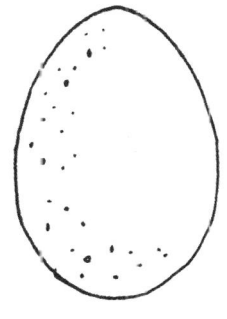

Eggs contain vitamin **B2**.

Sardines contain vitamin **B3**.

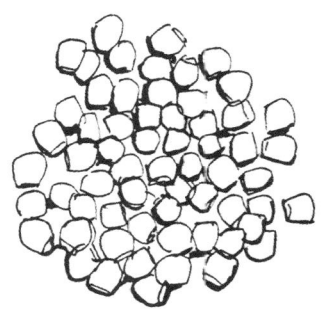

Sweetcorn contains vitamin **A**.

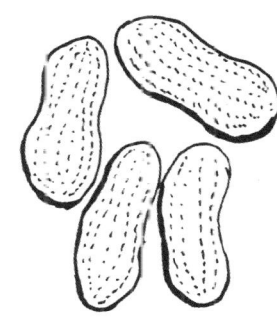

Peanuts contain vitamin **E**.

Bananas contain vitamin **K**.

Sunflower seeds contain vitamin **B1**.

Prawns contain vitamin **B2**.

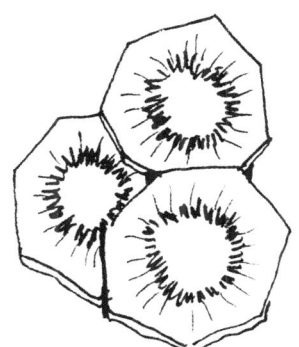

Kiwi fruit contain vitamin **B3**.

EATING AND DIGESTION

FOOD'S JOURNEY

Food is pushed through your digestive system by waves of squeezing and relaxing muscles. This is called peristalsis.

In your oesophagus, peristalsis is so strong it even works if your body is upside down!

QUICK FACTS

The digestive system starts at the **MOUTH** and ends at the anus.

Without food inside, most of the digestive passageway would be squeezed **FLAT** by the natural pressure of other organs.

Food has to be pushed through the passageway by waves of muscle action in its walls, called **PERISTALSIS**.

In adults, the digestive system is about **29 FT** long.

Food can take anything from 10–20 hours to **PASS THROUGH** the system.

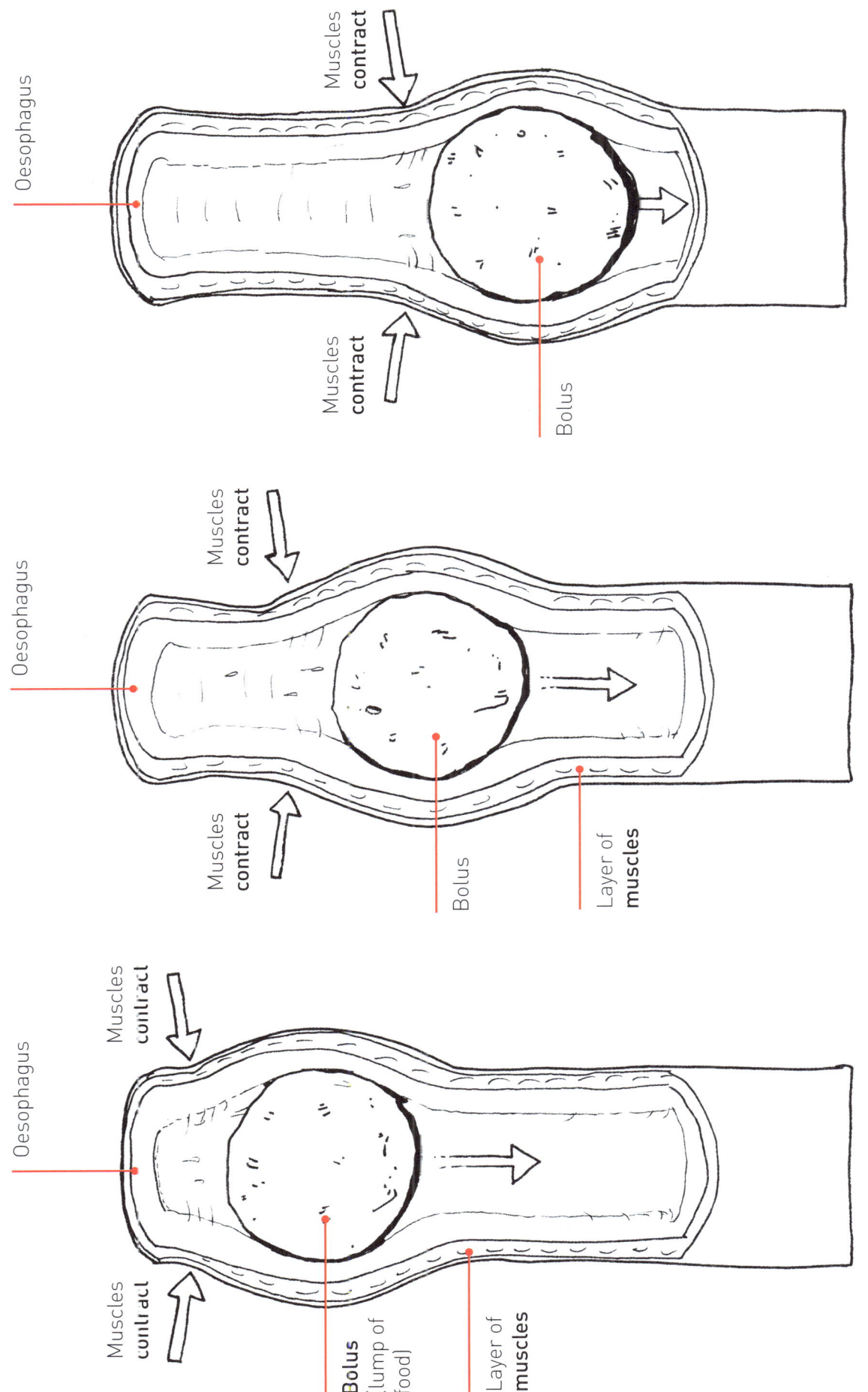

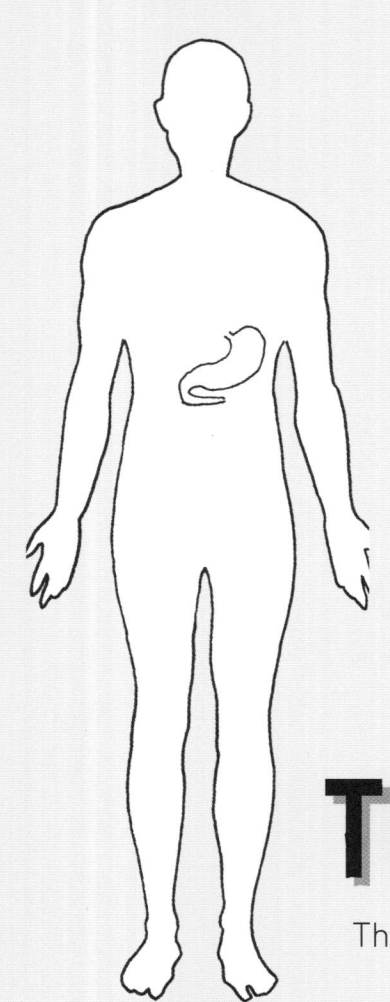

THE STOMACH

The stomach is like a stretchy storage bag for food. It expands to hold a whole meal.

The layers of muscle in its walls contract to make it squeeze first one way and then the other. Meanwhile, tiny glands in the stomach lining release their digestive chemicals.

After a few hours the food has become a mushy, part-digested soup.

QUICK FACTS

The stomach is a J-shaped **BAG** behind the left lower ribs.

Its lining makes thick **MUCUS** to protect the stomach's gastric juices from digesting the stomach itself.

An adult stomach can hold as much as **2.5 PINTS** of food.

If you did not have a stomach you could not eat just two or three main **MEALS** a day. You would have to eat lots of tiny ones much more frequently.

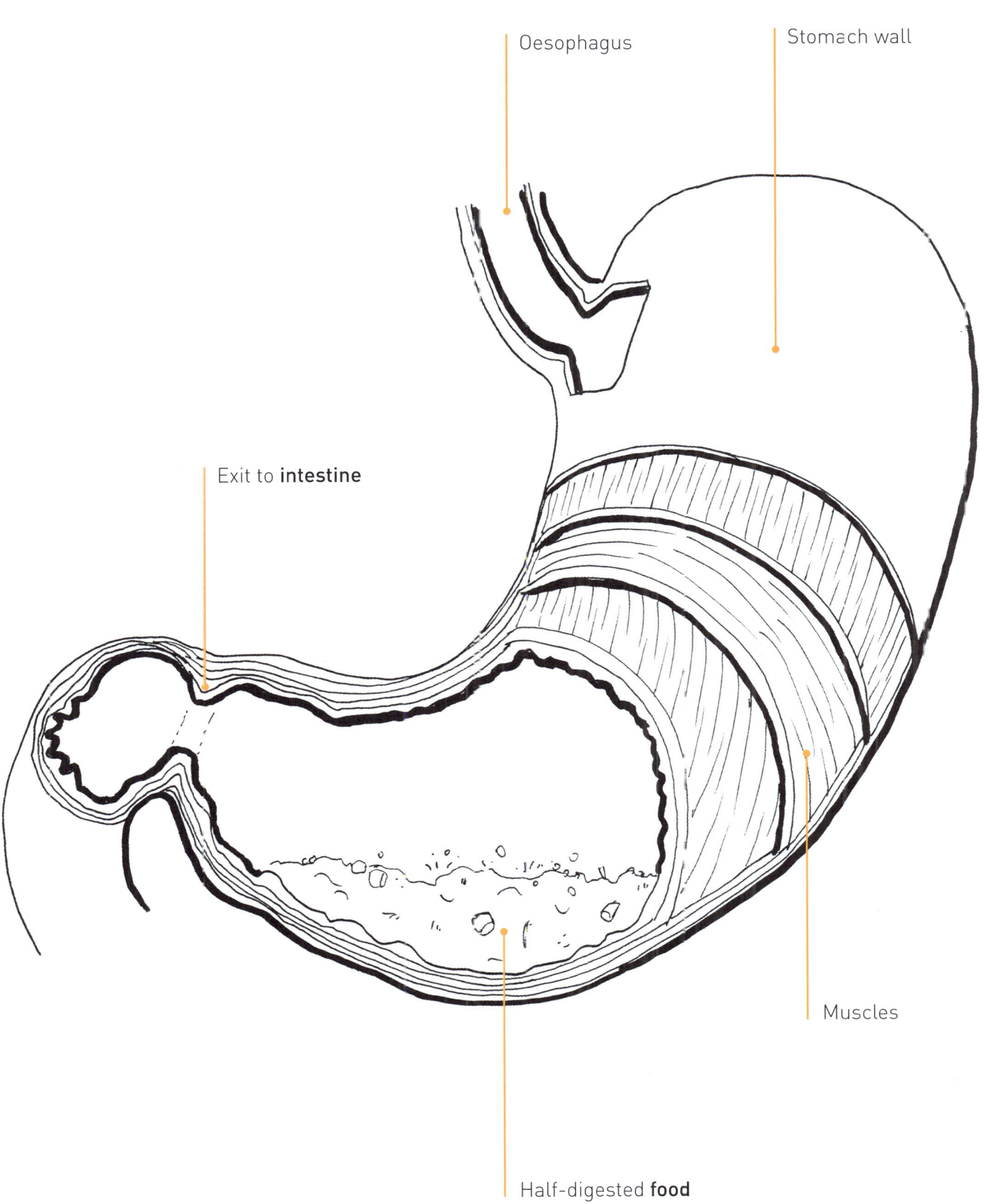

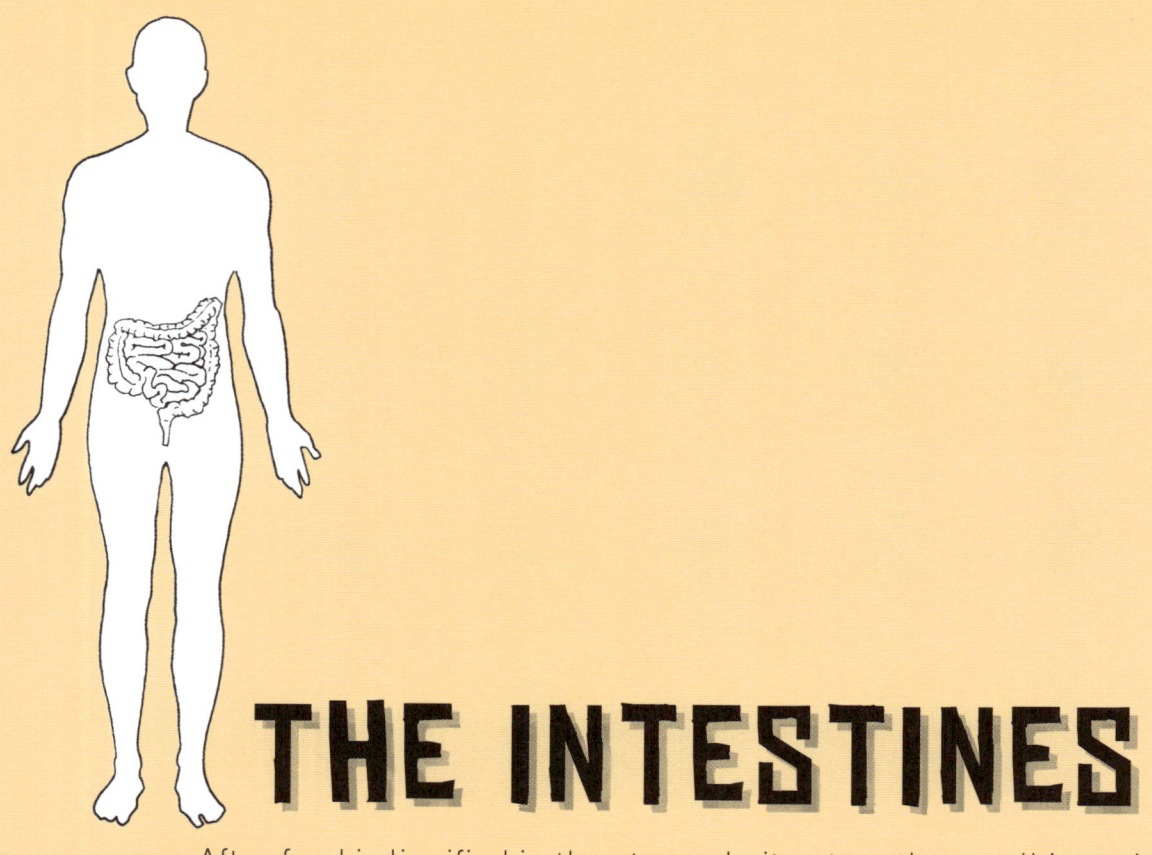

THE INTESTINES

After food is liquified in the stomach, it enters the small intestine.

In the first part of the small intestine, digestion continues. Juices from the pancreas and liver help to further break down the foods. It is also in the small intestine that digested food is absorbed into the blood and lymph.

Finally, in the large intestine, water is absorbed and the contents become more solid, so they can leave the body as waste material.

QUICK FACTS

The small intestine is about 7.6 yards long and is lined with small, finger-like nodules called **VILLI**.

Food particles are small enough to pass through the walls of the intestine and blood vessels only when they are completely **DIGESTED**.

Almost no digestion occurs in the large intestine. Its function is to **STORE** waste food products, and **ABSORB** water and small amounts of minerals.

The **WASTE** that accumulates in the large intestine is fibrous material that cannot be digested.

THERE ARE ABOUT 500 MILLION VILLI IN THE BODY.

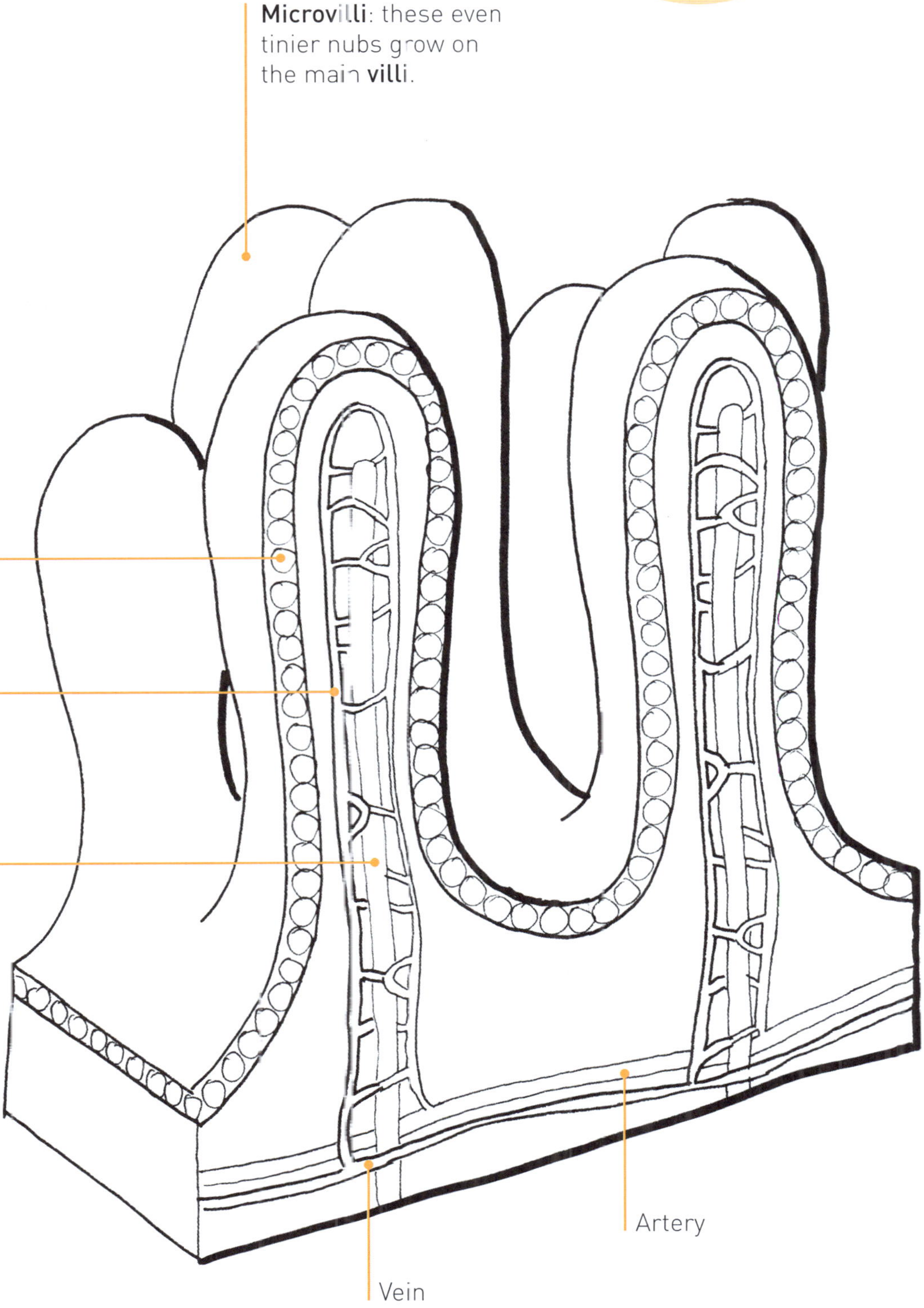

Microvilli: these even tinier nubs grow on the main **villi**.

Thin walls: just one **cell** thick.

Network of **capillaries**

Lacteal

Artery

Vein

EATING AND DIGESTION 61

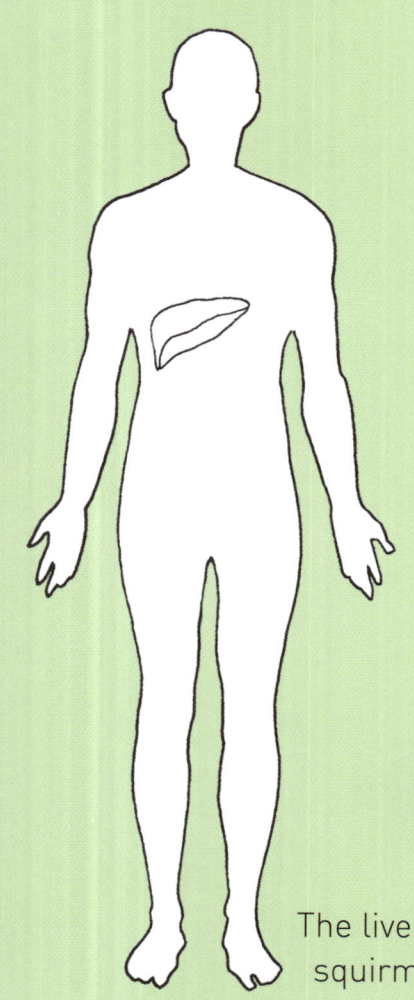

THE LIVER

The liver is one of the body's busiest parts. It does not squirm about or move, like the stomach, intestines, heart, or muscles. Its activities are invisible.

The liver has two key roles to play: making (or processing) new chemicals, and neutralizing poisons and waste products.

QUICK FACTS

The liver is the **LARGEST** single part, or organ, inside the body.

It plays an essential role in the **STORAGE** of certain vitamins.

The liver has more than 500 known **TASKS** in the body, and probably more that have not yet been discovered.

The liver is so busy with chemical processes and tasks that it makes lots of **HEAT**.

Usually the liver **BREAKS DOWN** old red blood cells and gets rid of the coloring substance in bile fluid.

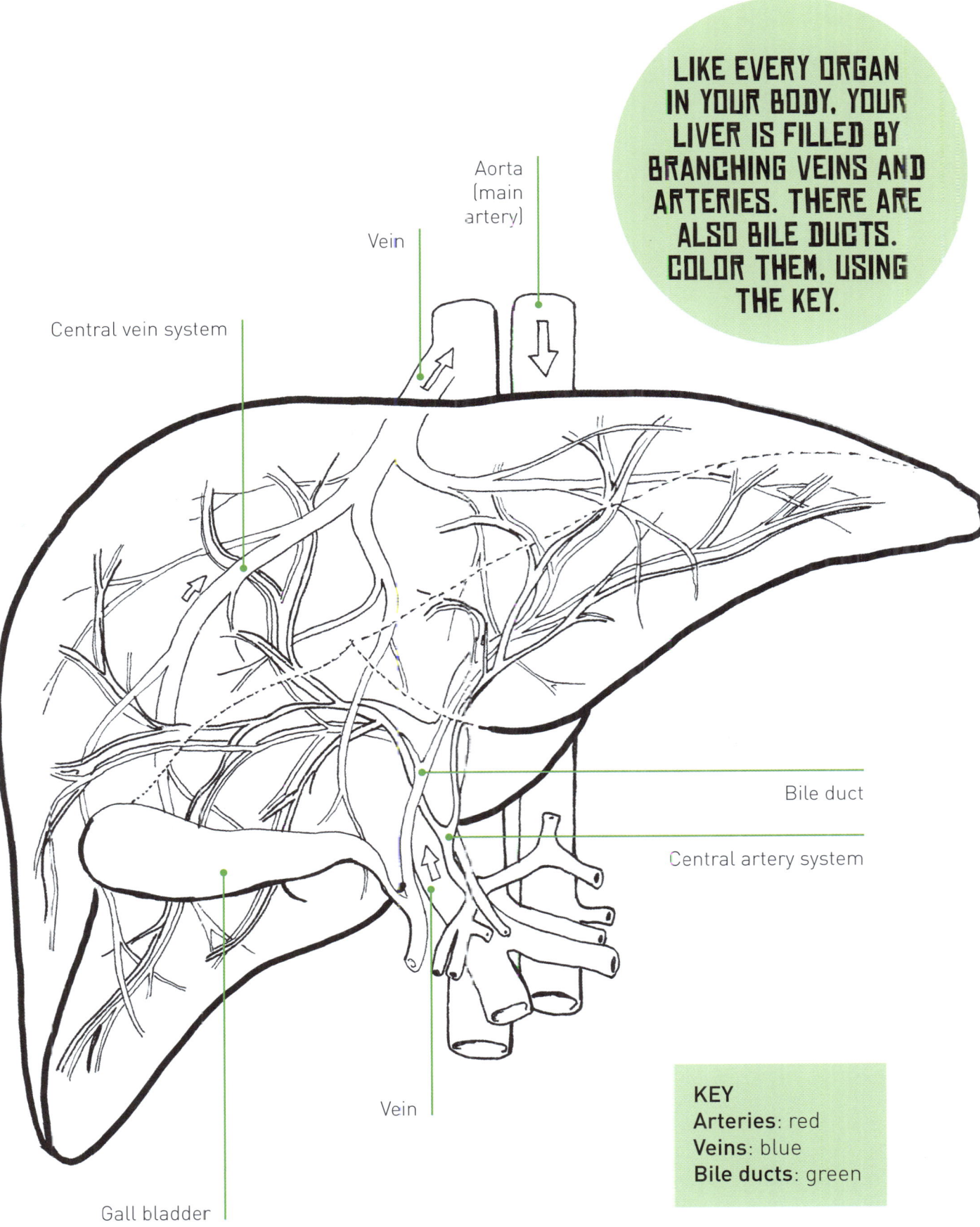

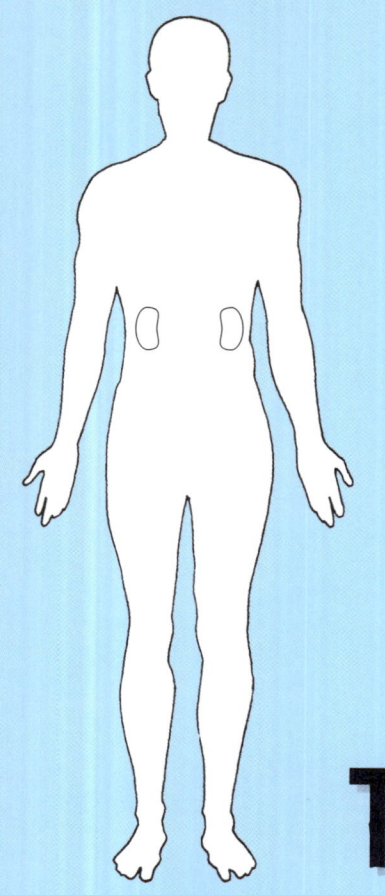

THE KIDNEYS

The removal of waste materials from the body is known as excretion, and the body's main organs of excretion are the kidneys.

Kidneys clean the blood by filtering out waste and straining off any water the body doesn't need. This liquid waste is called urine. It is stored in your bladder and then leaves your body when you go to the toilet.

QUICK FACTS

You have **TWO** kidneys, in the small of your back, one on either side of your backbone.

They look like large, reddish-brown **BEANS**, and each one is about the size of a clenched fist.

Your kidneys filter about **500 GALLONS** of blood daily.

The kidneys receive a **HUGE** blood supply through the renal arteries and veins.

The **ADRENAL GLANDS** are attached to the kidneys. They help create energy which stimulates the body to prepare it for instant action.

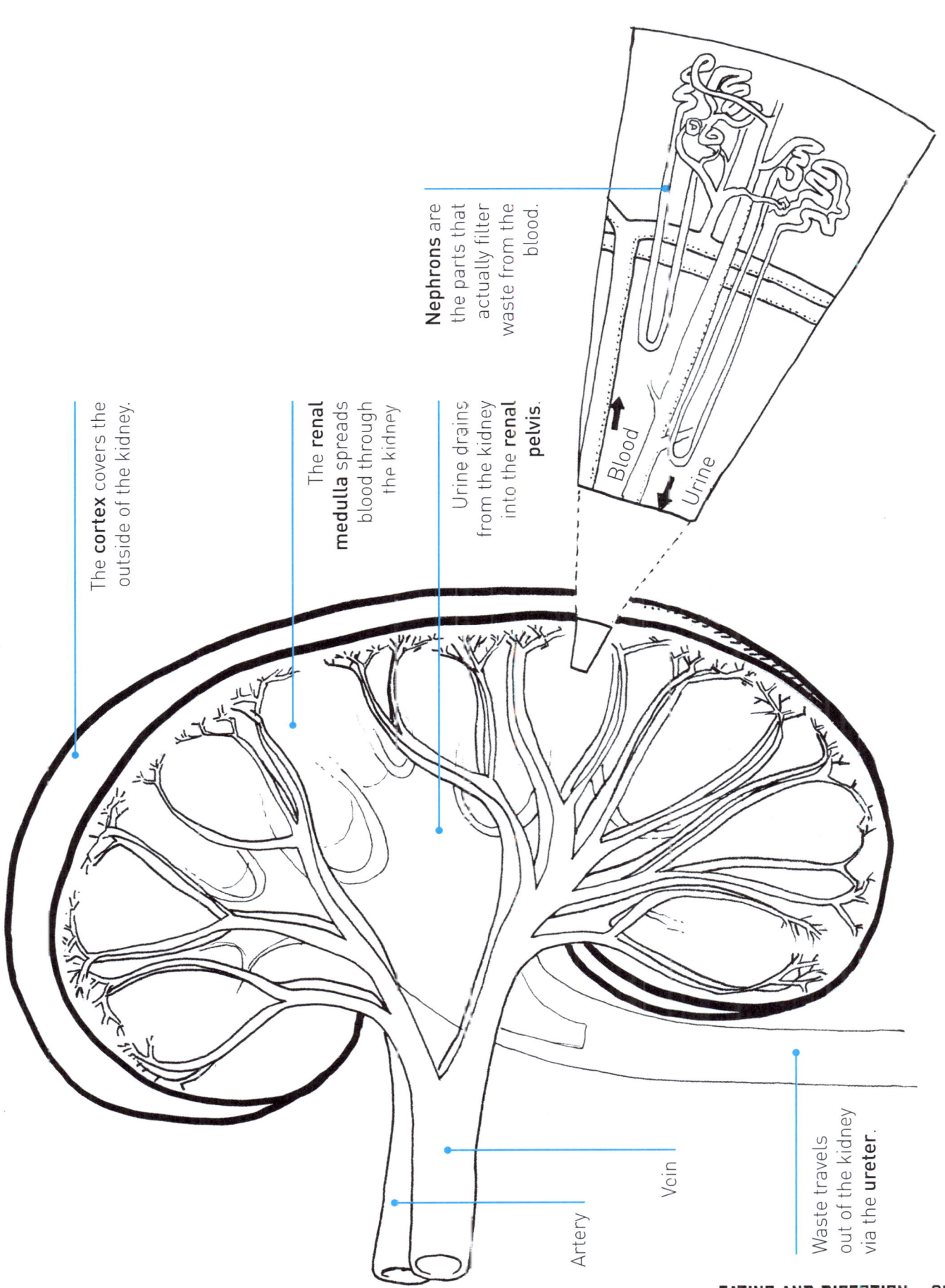

EATING AND DIGESTION 65

SENSES

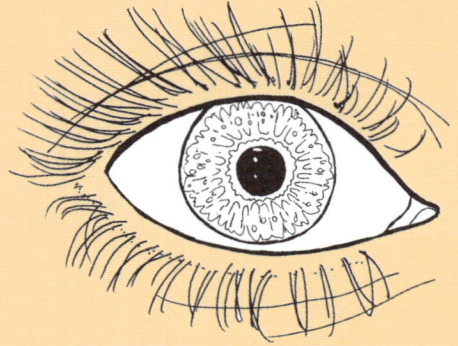 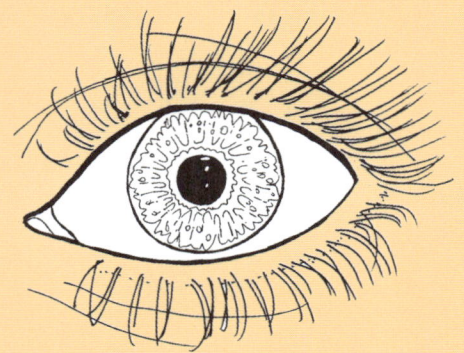

THE EYES

The eye is very like a camera. It has an adjustable opening to let in the light (the pupil), a lens that focuses the light to form an image, and a sensitive film (the retina) on which the image is recorded.

Inside each human eye are about 130 billion light-sensitive cells. When light falls on one of these cells it causes a chemical change. This change starts an impulse in the eye fiber which sends a message through the optic nerve to the "seeing" part of your brain.

QUICK FACTS

The human eye is so **SENSITIVE** that a person sitting on top of a hill on a moonless night could see a match being struck up to 50 miles away.

BIRDS have the keenest sight of all animals, including human beings. An osprey can see a dead animal on the ground from a height of up to 20 miles.

Each **EYEBALL** sits in a bony bowl called the eye socket. It is formed by curved parts of five skull bones.

The eye is one of the body parts that **GROWS** least from birth to adulthood.

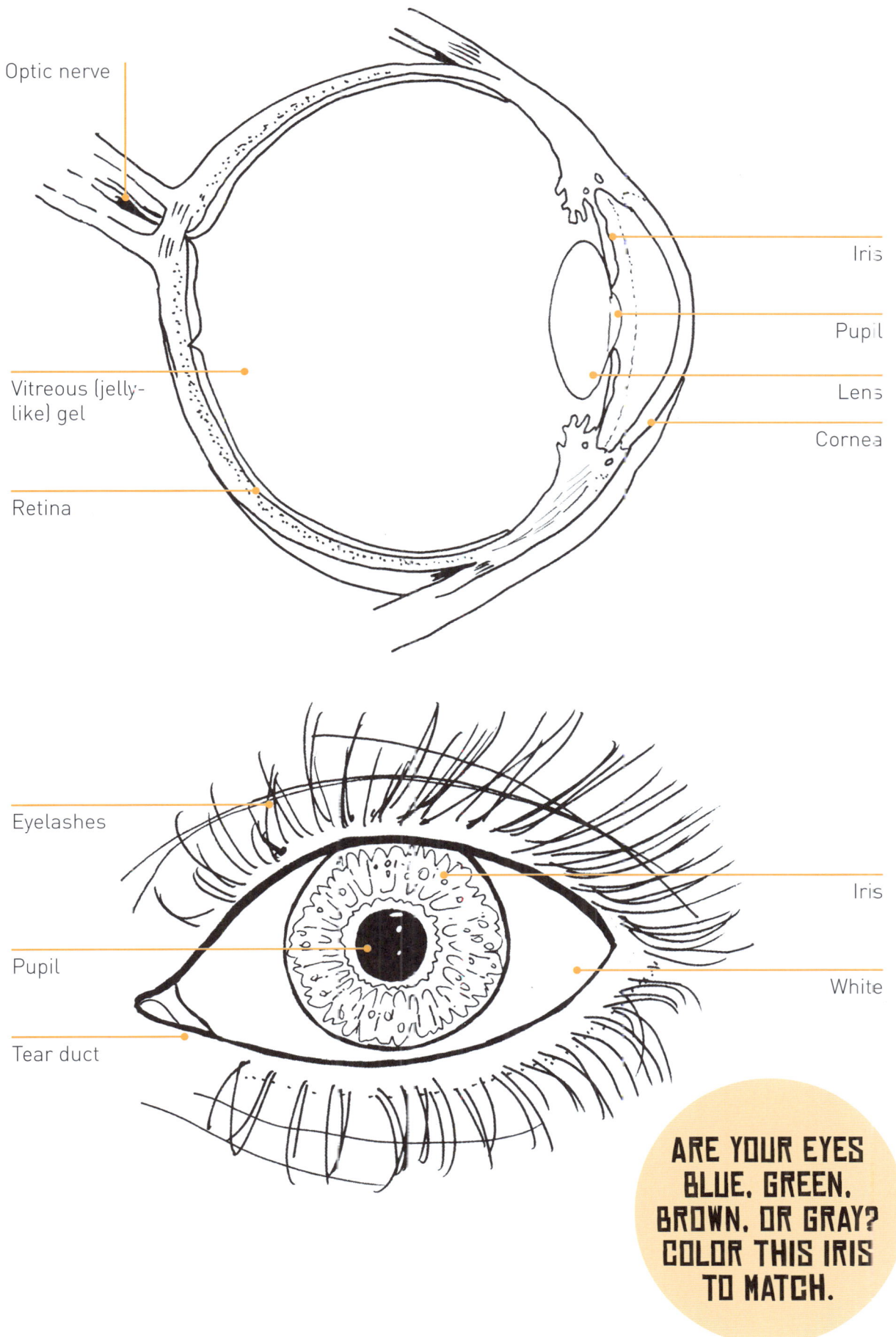

ARE YOUR EYES BLUE, GREEN, BROWN, OR GRAY? COLOR THIS IRIS TO MATCH.

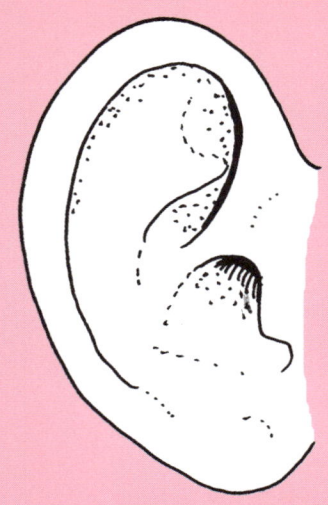

THE EARS

Hearing involves much more than the ears on the side of your head. These are the outer ears or ear flaps, made of skin-covered cartilage. The inner ear is deep in the temporal skull bone, almost behind the eye.

The ear is actually made up of three parts: outer, middle, and inner.

QUICK FACTS

When you fly in a plane your ears may **POP** as the air inside them expands. Otherwise, your eardrum would burst as the air trapped inside your ear expanded.

The middle and inner ears are **PROTECTED** from knocks by skull bones.

A sound from **ONE SIDE** reaches the ear on that side more than 1,000th of a second before it reaches the other ear.

The brain "**BLOCKS OUT**" frequent noise like humming machinery. Only when we hear something **NEW** does the mind turn its attention to hearing.

We never see lightning and hear **THUNDER** at the same time. This is because light travels faster than sound.

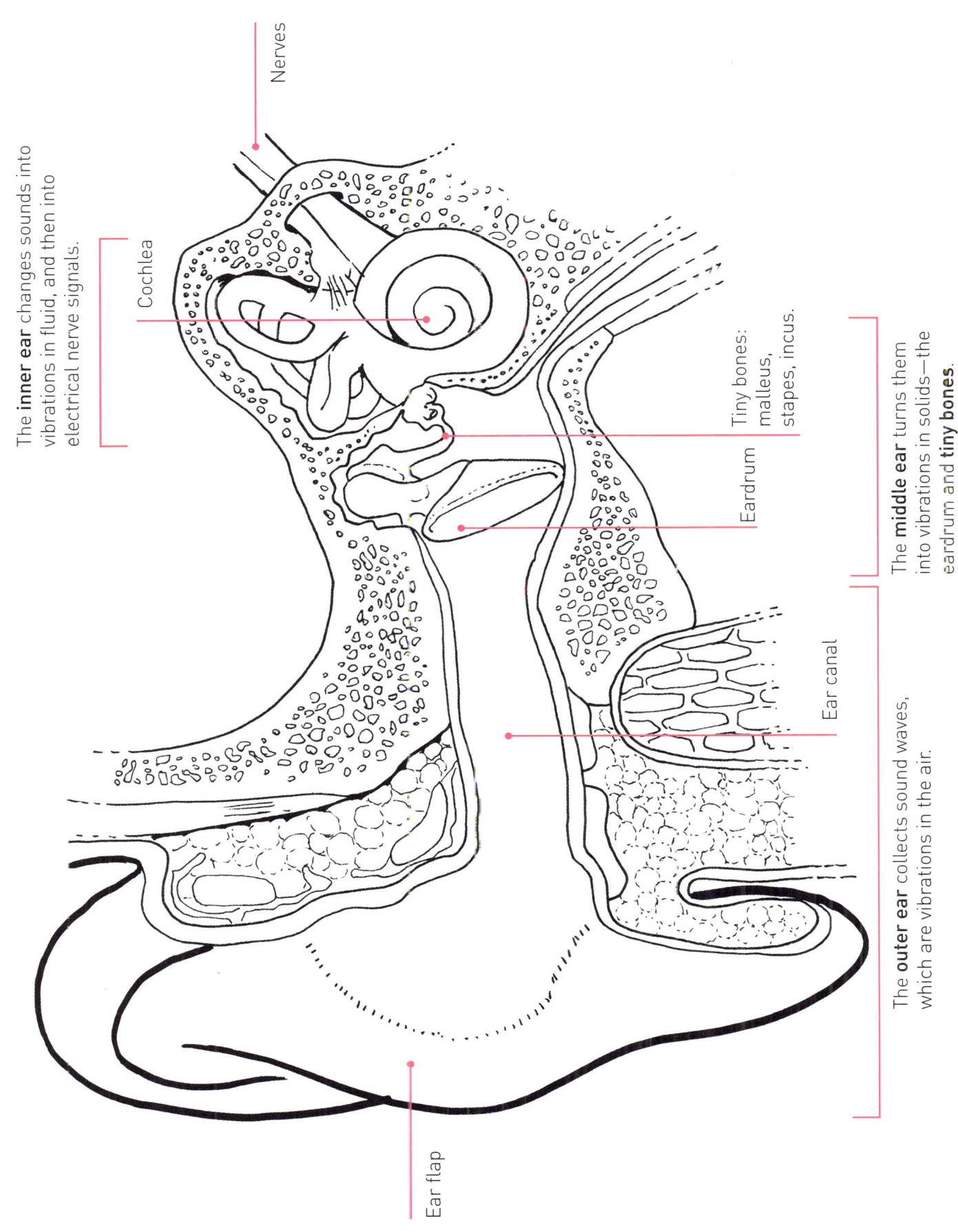

SENSES 71

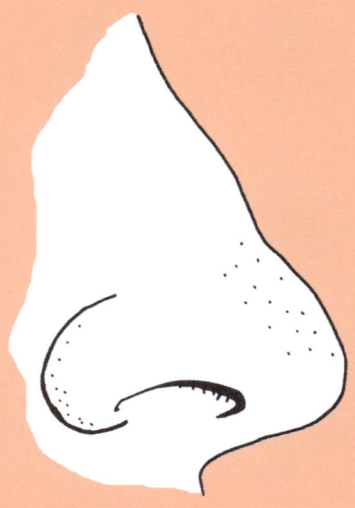

THE NOSE

As you breathe in, air passes through a cavity behind your nose, which contains patches of millions of smell receptors. Sensory hairs stick out from the surface of these cells. The hairs detect smells and pass information along nerve fibers to the brain.

Substances that you can recognize as having an odor dissolve in the layer of mucus covering the sensory cells, stimulating them to produce a signal.

QUICK FACTS

The little hairs in the nose also **CLEAN** the air we inhale, as well as warming it before it enters the body.

The **OLFACTORY** (smelling) patch in the top of the nasal chamber has about the same area as a thumbnail.

Most people are able to detect about **4,000** different smells.

People whose work is based on their ability to smell, such as chefs, perfume makers, and wine tasters, can distinguish as many as **10,000** different smells.

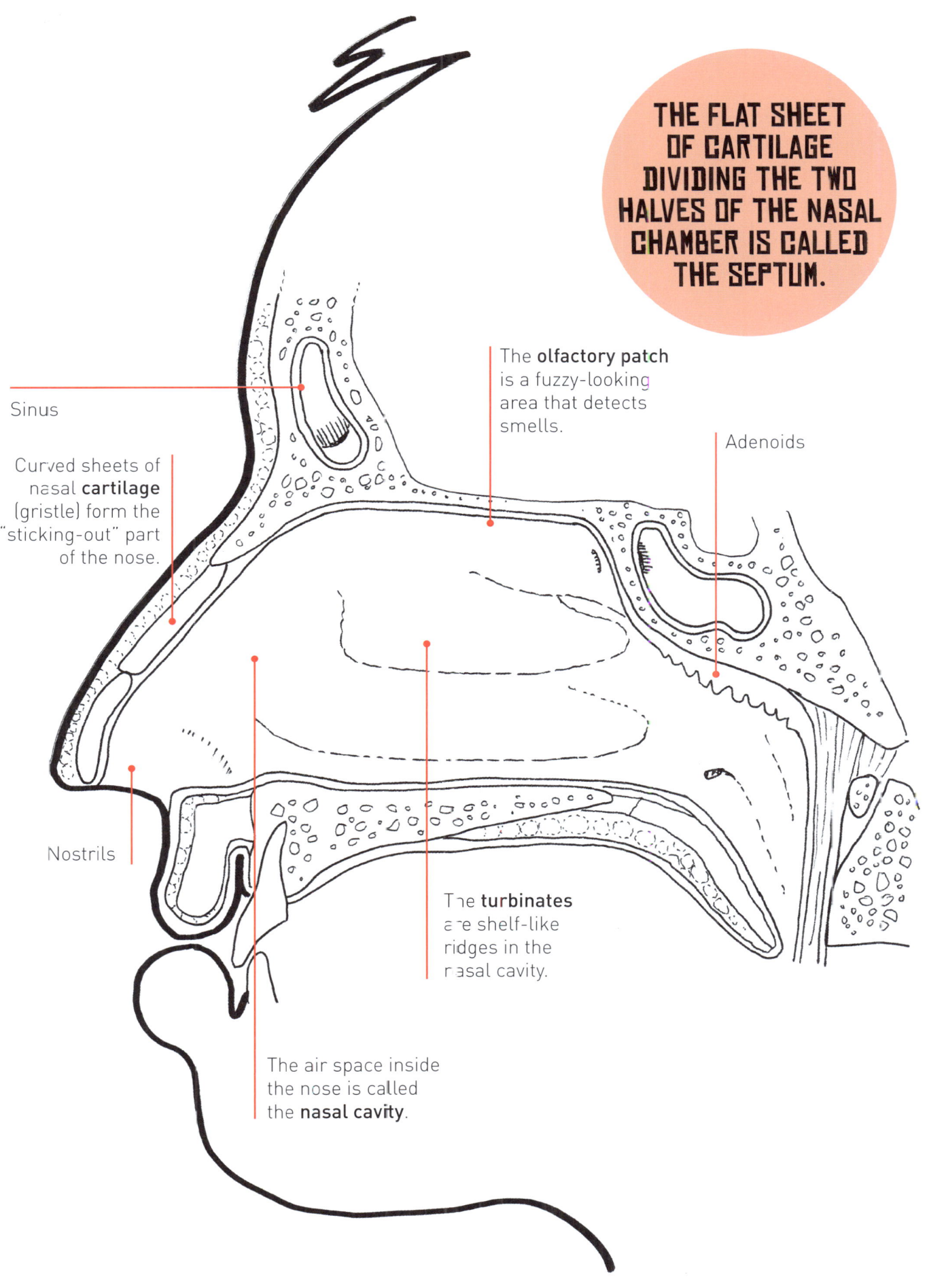

SENSES 73

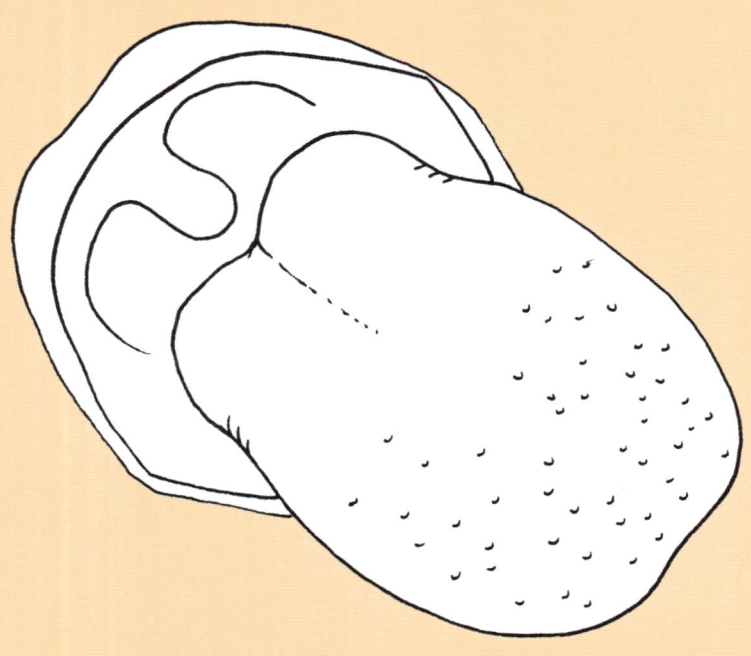

THE TONGUE

The tongue is the body's most flexible muscle. It has 12 sections of muscles inside it, and goes from long and thin, when poking out, to short and wide at the back of the mouth, in less than a second.

The tongue helps with chewing and swallowing, and also with the formation of words.

QUICK FACTS

We sense different basic **FLAVORS** on different parts of the tongue.

The four main **TASTES** are sweet, salt, sour, and bitter.

You can **CHECK** where the four tastes are by dabbing your tongue with a little salt, sugar, coffee grounds (bitter), and lemon juice (sour).

A fifth taste, **UMAMI**, has also been recognized in recent years, and relates to the Japanese word for "savory".

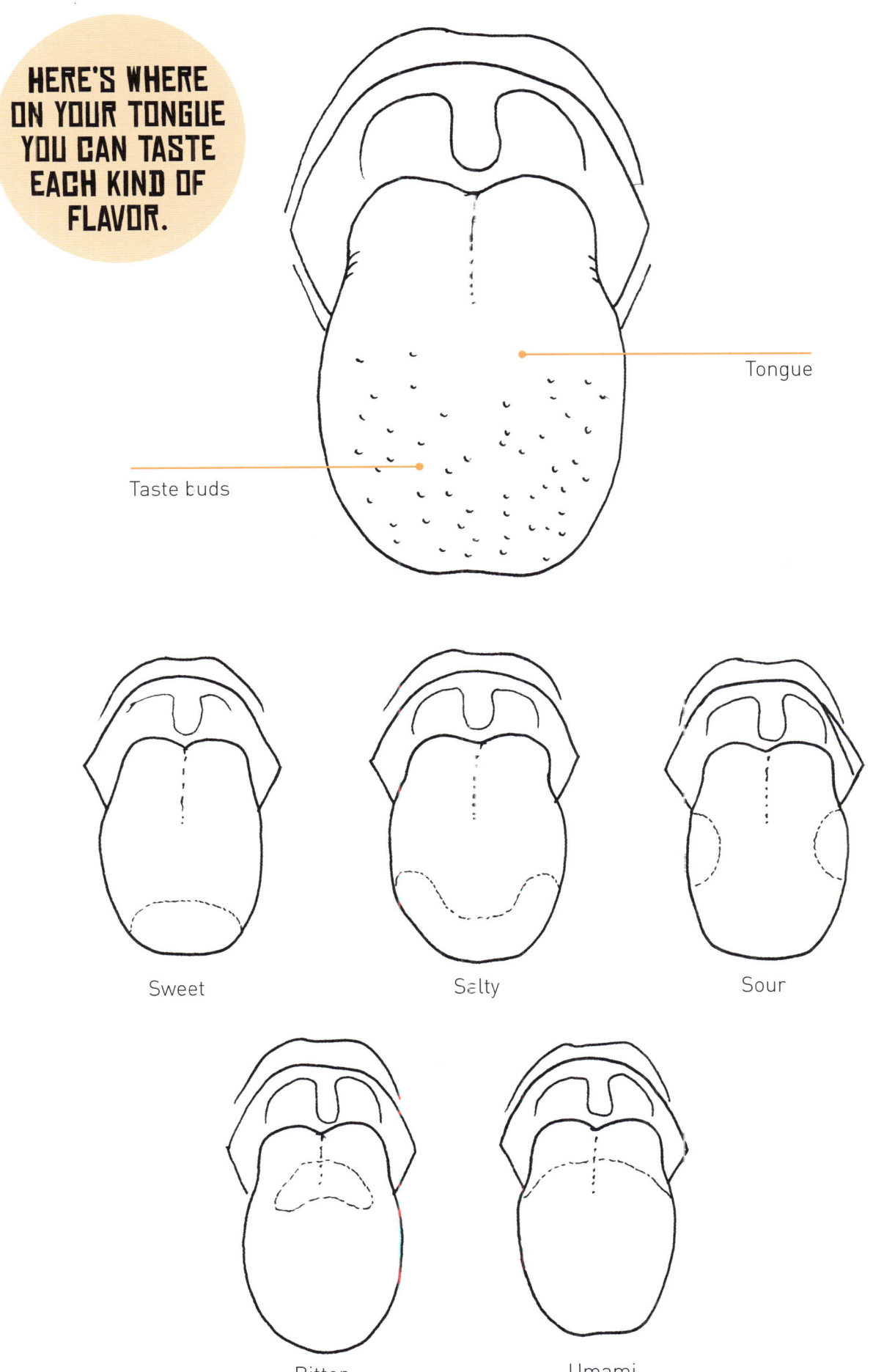

HERE'S WHERE ON YOUR TONGUE YOU CAN TASTE EACH KIND OF FLAVOR.

Tongue

Taste buds

Sweet

Salty

Sour

Bitter

Umami

SENSES

TOUCH

Senses in the skin are measured by tiny receptors at the ends of nerves. There are several different types of receptor. Each type can detect only one kind of sensation, such as pain, temperature, pressure, touch, and so on.

QUICK FACTS

Without this constant flow of information, you would keep **INJURING** yourself accidentally, which is what happens in some rare diseases where the skin senses are lost.

The hands are among the body's most **SENSITIVE** parts.

Skin on the **FINGERTIPS** has the most microsensors, providing the most sensitive touch.

A "**TOUCH TYPIST**" is able to operate computer keys without actually looking at them.

Your sense of touch is more complicated than it seems. It's not just a single sense, detecting physical contact. It's a "multi-sense", detecting:

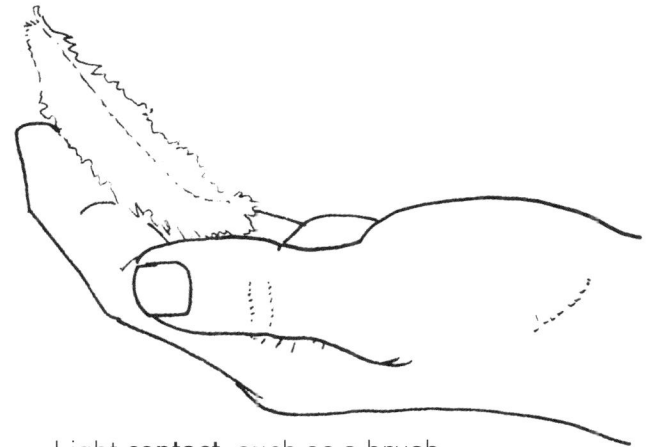

Light **contact**, such as a brush from a feather.

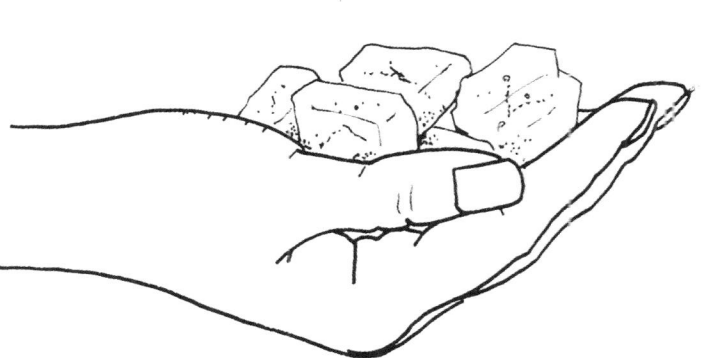

Cold, like an ice cube.

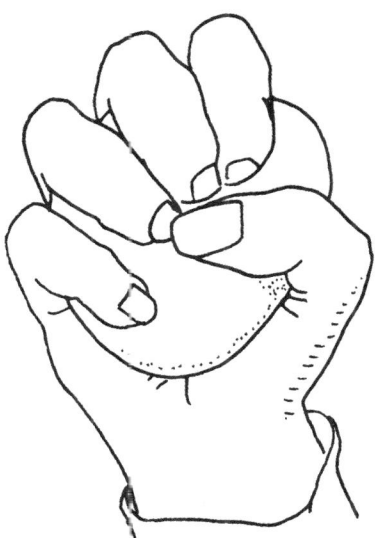

Heavy **pressure**, such as being squeezed hard.

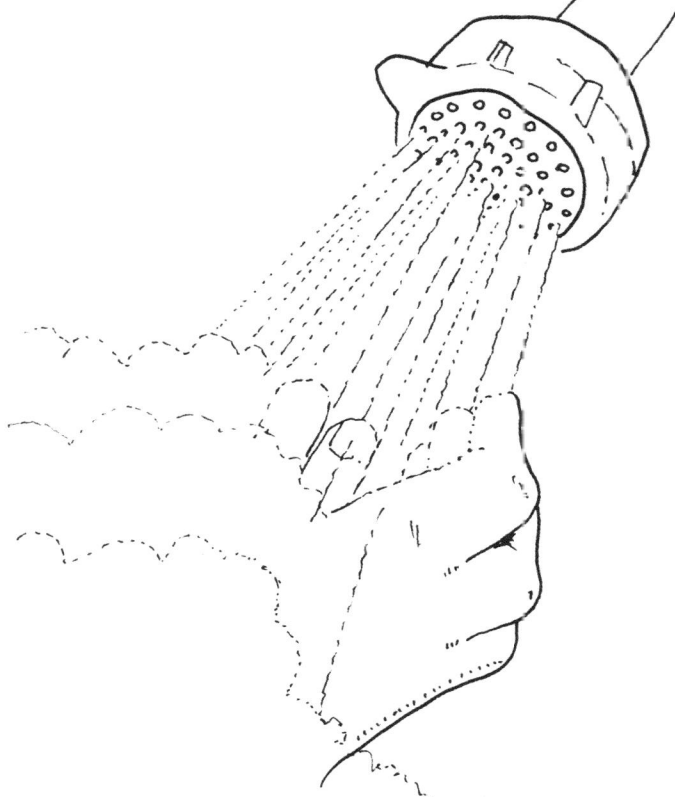

Movement: your skin can detect movements that are too small for your eye to see.

Surface texture, such as rough wood or smooth plastic.

Moisture content, from dry sand to wet mud.

Heat, such as a hot shower or bath.

SENSES 77

BONES

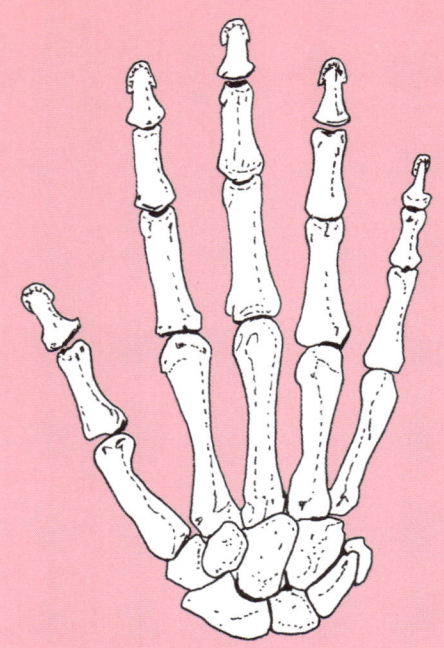

WHAT IS BONE?

A typical bone is actually made of two types of tissue. On the outside is a type of "skin" called the periosteum. Below this is a thin layer of thick, dense, "solid" bone. It is known as hard or compact bony tissue.

Inside this, and forming the bulk of the middle of the bone, is spongy tissue, which has gaps and spaces in it like honeycomb. It is much lighter than the outer compact bone, and the spaces are filled with blood vessels and jelly-like bone marrow for making new blood cells.

QUICK FACTS

More than 99 per cent of the body's **CALCIUM** is contained in the bones and teeth.

Most bones of the skeleton begin in a baby not as real bone, but as a slightly softer, bendier, smooth substance called **CARTILAGE** (gristle).

The nose and ears are mainly cartilage, not true bone, which is why they are slightly **BENDY**.

Even in the **ADULT** skeleton, some bones remain partly cartilage.

BONE ALSO CONTAINS THREAD-LIKE FIBERS OF COLLAGEN, WHICH MAKE IT SLIGHTLY BENDY UNDER PRESSURE.

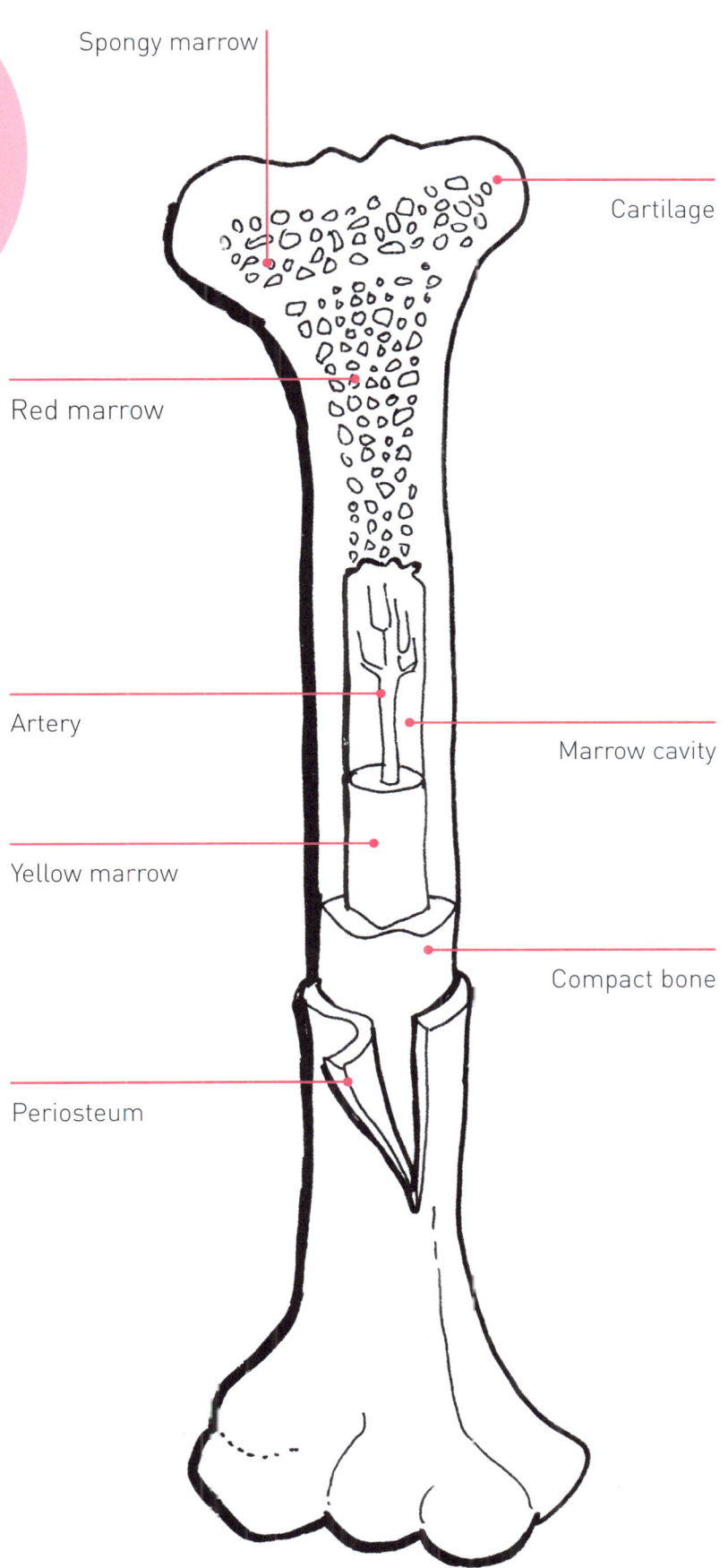

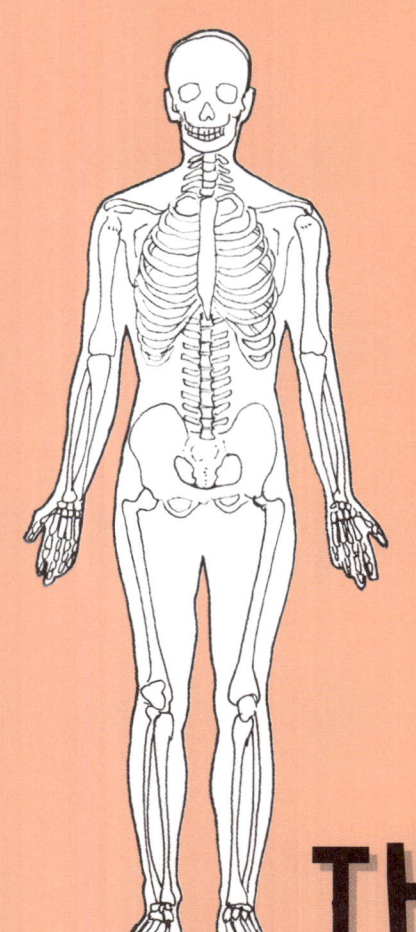

THE SKELETON

A skeleton is made up of a network of bones, providing a frame that holds the whole body together.

Around and under your skeleton is connective tissue, which acts as support, and binds the bones together. It tethers the larger organs to keep them in place, and provides softness for protection.

QUICK FACTS

At **BIRTH**, a baby has 300 bones, but 94 join together in early childhood.

A human skeleton contains, on average, **206** bones.

The skeleton protects delicate **ORGANS** such as the brain, heart, and lungs.

It provides a system of levers that the **MUSCLES** can work on, enabling us to move.

Your **HAND** and **WRIST** alone contain 27 bones.

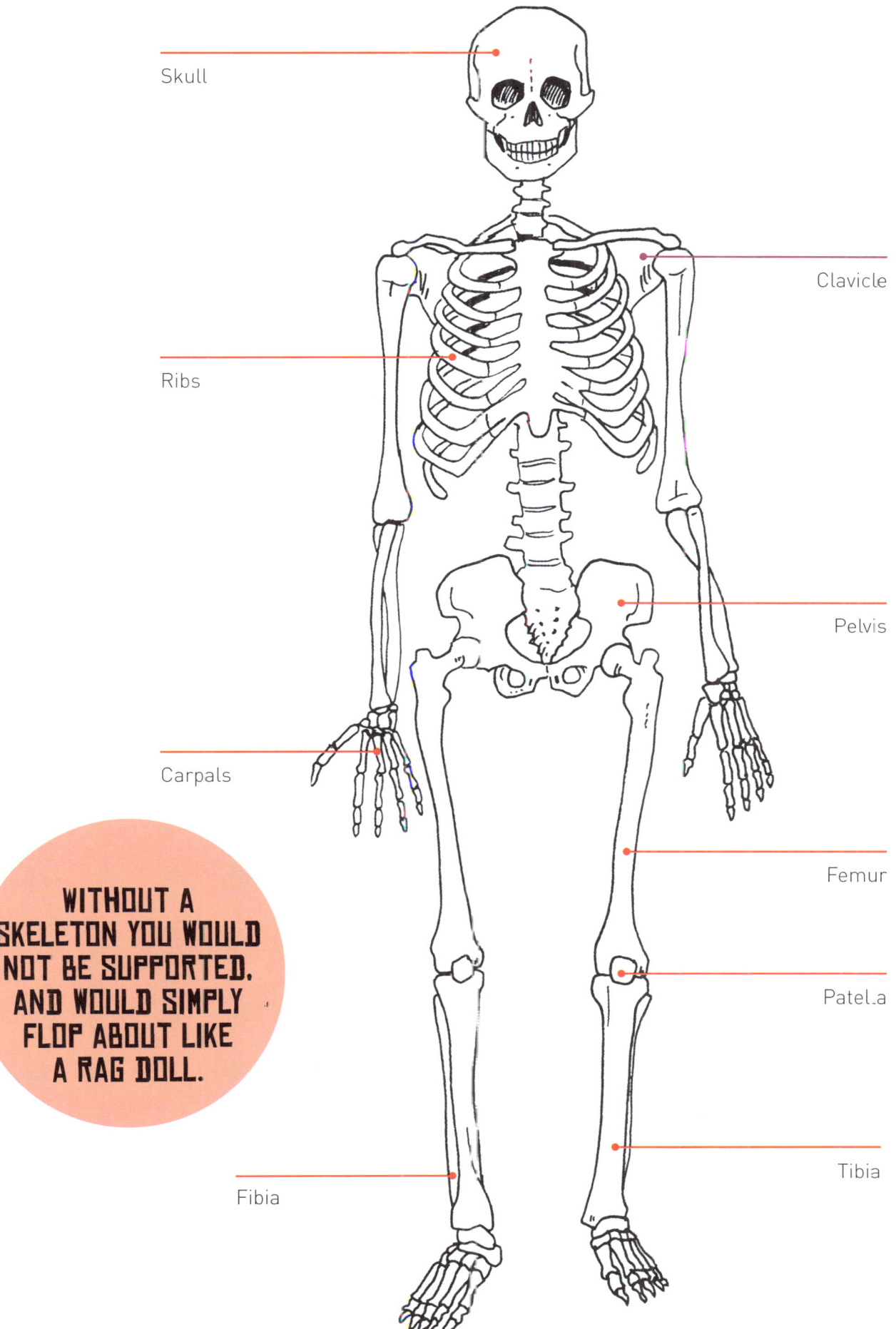

- Skull
- Clavicle
- Ribs
- Pelvis
- Carpals
- Femur
- Patella
- Fibia
- Tibia

WITHOUT A SKELETON YOU WOULD NOT BE SUPPORTED, AND WOULD SIMPLY FLOP ABOUT LIKE A RAG DOLL.

BONES 63

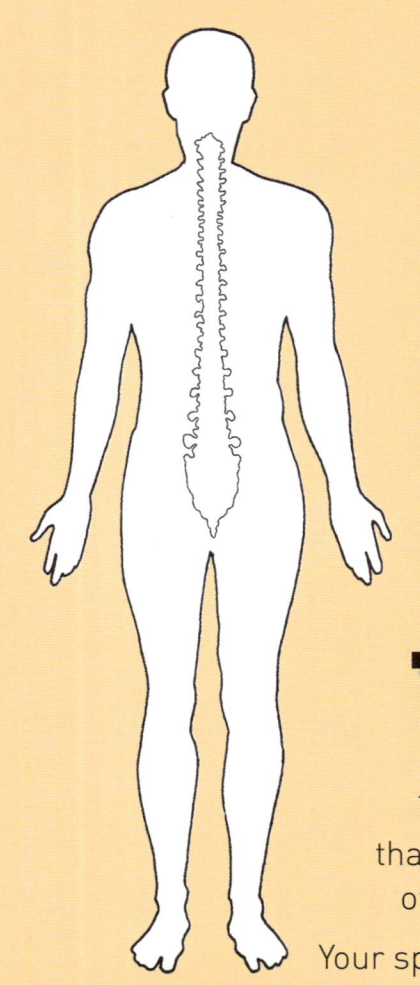

THE SPINE

The spine is the part of the skeleton that extends down the back. It is made up of a column of bones called vertebrae.

Your spine plays an important role in posture and movement, and it also protects your spinal cord.

The vertebrae are held in place by muscles and strong connective tissue called ligaments. Most of the vertebrae have fibrous discs between them to absorb shock and enable the spine to bend.

QUICK FACTS

The spine is also known as the **BACKBONE**.

The human spine consists of 33 **VERTEBRAE**, but some of them grow together in adults.

The spine normally has a slight natural **CURVE**.

Sometimes the intervertebral disc, the tissue that lies between the vertebrae, **STICKS OUT** and presses on nerves.

This condition is called a **SLIPPED DISC**. It can cause severe pain in the lower back, thighs, and legs.

84 HUMAN BODY

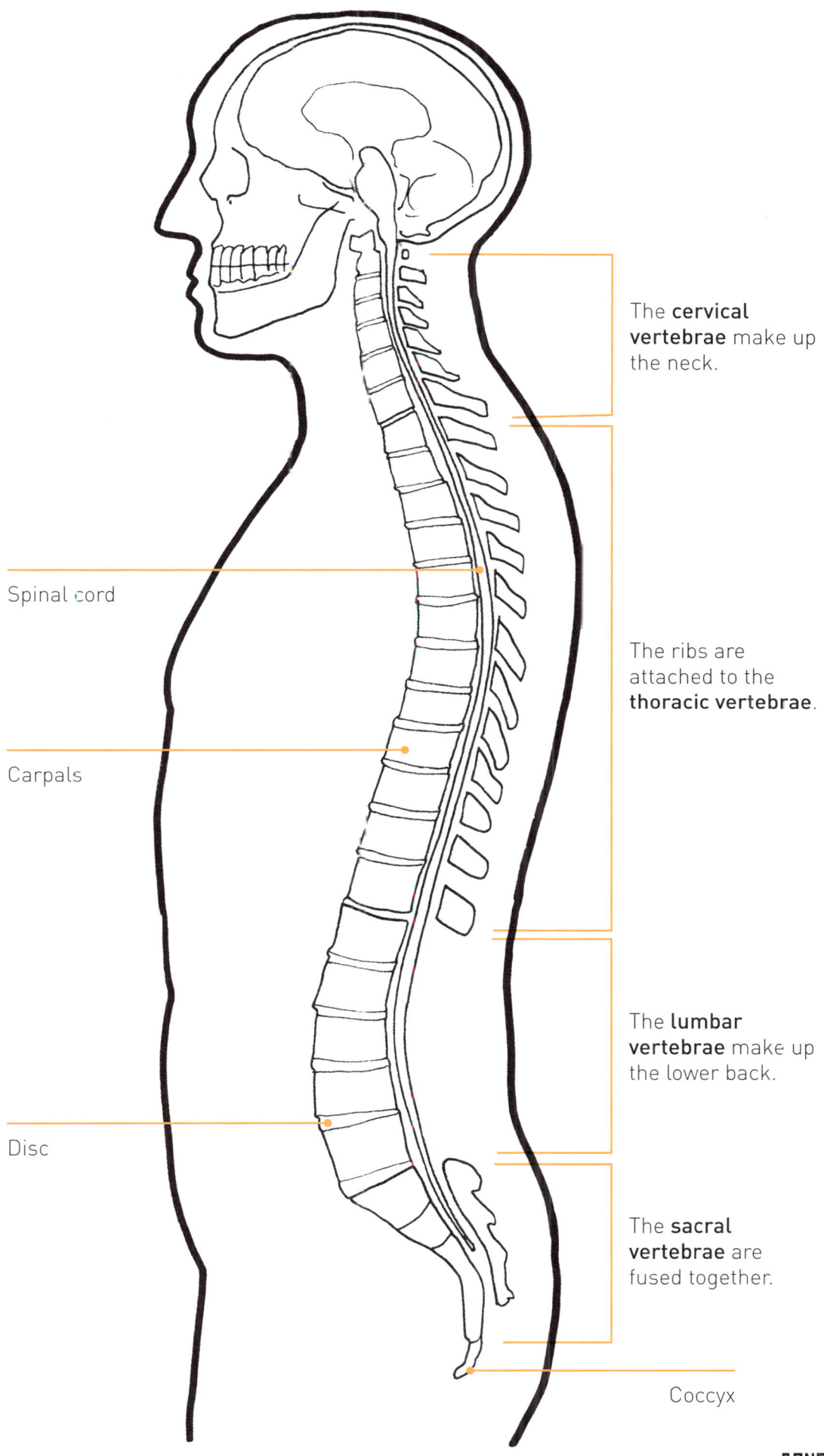

THE JOINTS

A joint is the meeting point between bones, and it usually controls the amount of movement. Some joints have to be strong, while others need to be very mobile.

As it is not possible for joints to be both strong and mobile, we require many different kinds of joints.

QUICK FACTS

Some joints move like a simple **HINGE**, such as those in the shoulder, elbows, and knees. A hinge joint allows extension and flexing.

Others move in **ALL DIRECTIONS**, such as the shoulder joint or the base of the thumb.

Joints in the **SPINE** allow only a small amount of movement.

Your muscles, bones, and joints together are known as the **MUSCULOSKELETAL** system.

Many joints are lubricated with an oily liquid called **SYNOVIAL FLUID** so they can bend freely.

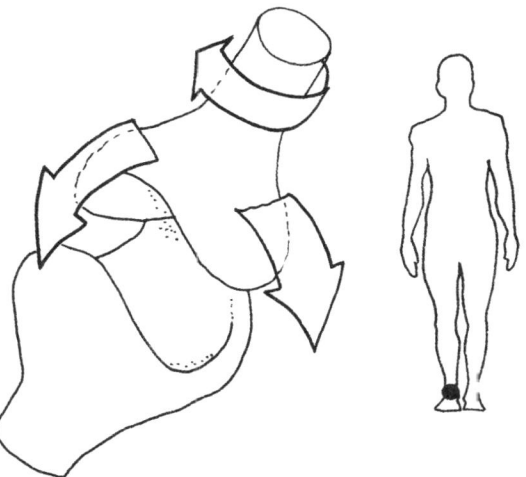

A **saddle** joint allows movement in two directions, but without rotation.

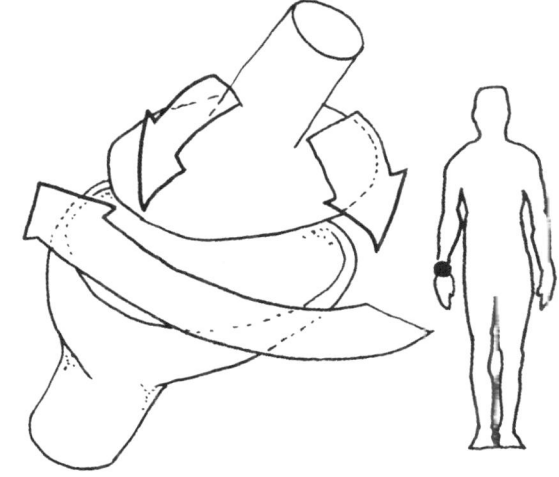

An **ellipsoid** joint allows circular and bending movement, but no rotation.

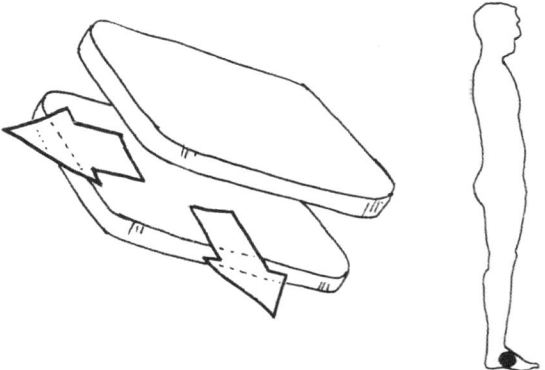

A **plane** joint has a flat surface that allows the bones to slide on each other, but they are restricted.

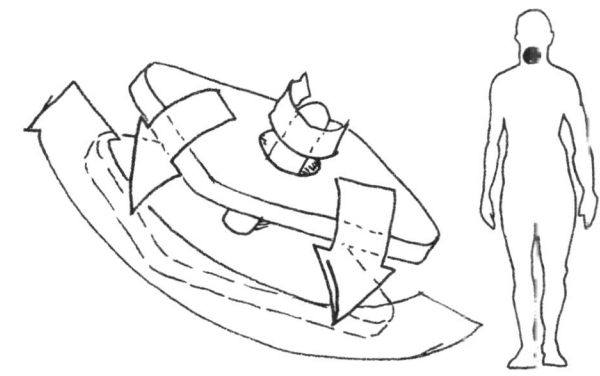

A **pivot** joint allows rotation, but no other movement.

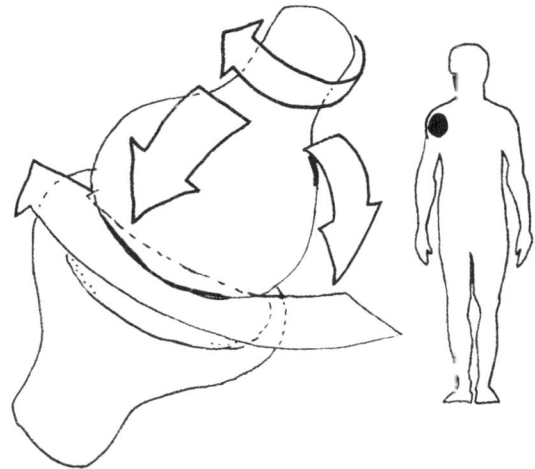

A **ball-and-socket** joint moves freely in all directions.

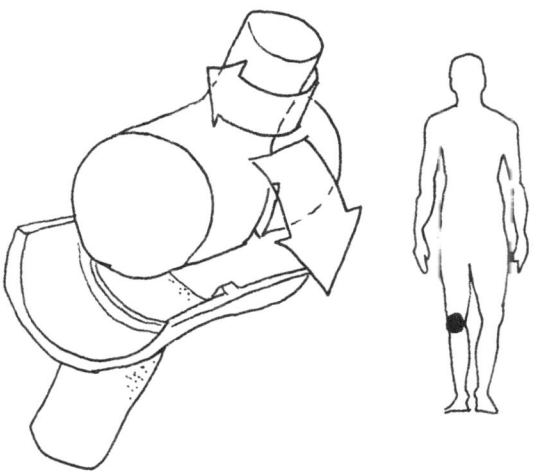

A **hinge** joint allows extension and flexing.

BONES 87

THE MUSCLES

There are 639 muscles in the human body, each comprising around 10 million muscle cells. Each of these cells is like a motor containing 10 cylinders arranged in a row.

The cylinders are tiny boxes that contain fluid, and when a muscle contracts, the brain sends a message to these tiny boxes.

QUICK FACTS

The human body has more than 600 **MAJOR** muscles. About 240 of them have specific names.

Most muscles can be controlled by **CONSCIOUSLY** thinking about them—they move when you want them to.

These are called **VOLUNTARY** muscles, and there are more than 600 of them in your body.

We use 200 voluntary muscles every time we take a **STEP**.

You use about 40 facial muscles to **FROWN**, but only half as many to smile. So save energy by smiling more!

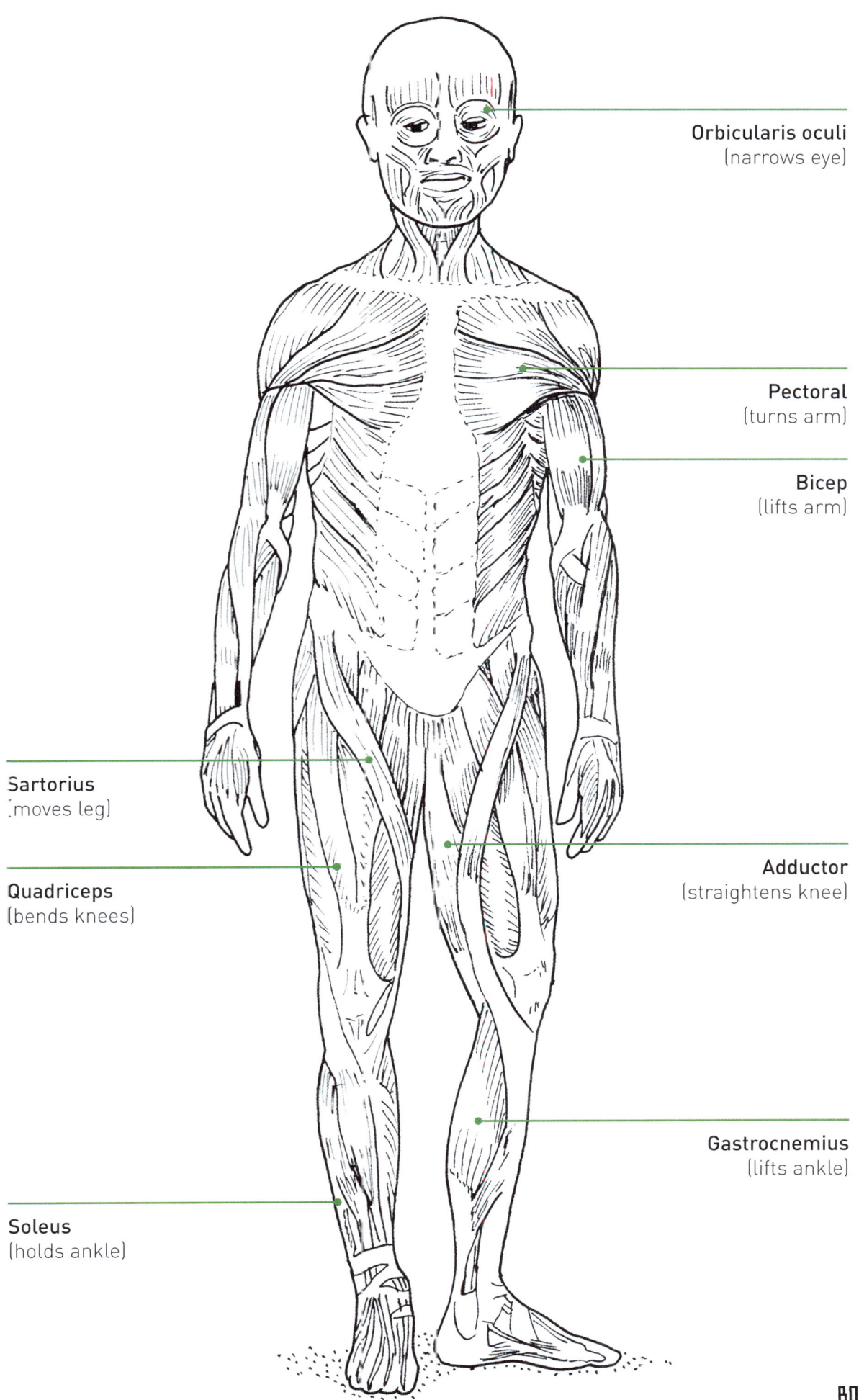

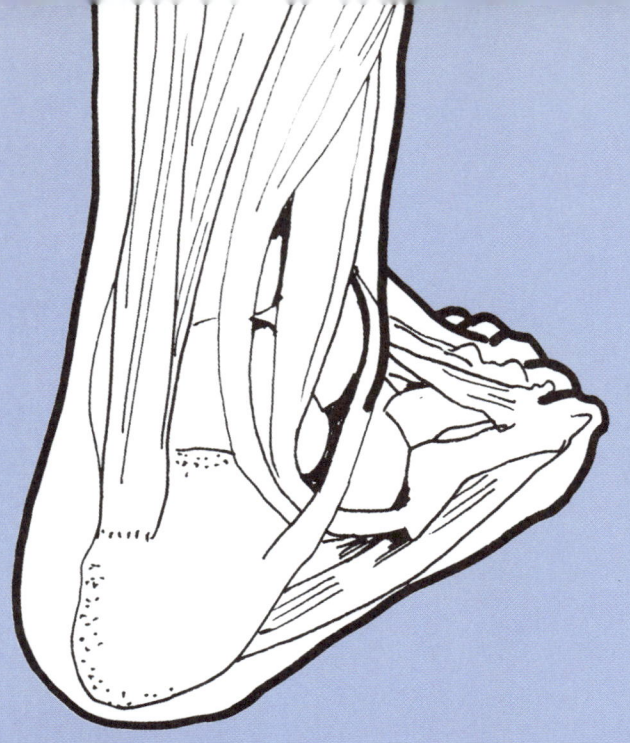

TENDONS

A tendon is a strong white cord that attaches muscles to bones. Muscles move bones by pulling on tendons. Some tendons are round, others are long and flat.

One end of a tendon rises from the end of a muscle, and the other end is woven into the substance of a bone. The tendon may slide up and down inside a sheath of fibrous tissue, in the same way that an arm moves in a coat sleeve.

QUICK FACTS

Tendons are also known as **SINEWS**.

Tendons at the ankle and wrist are enclosed in **SHEATHS** at the points where they cross or are in close contact with other structures.

CONNECTIVE TISSUE is a jelly-like material that binds tendons, muscles, and bones together.

The name "**ACHILLES TENDON**" comes from the legend of Achilles, a Greek hero killed by an arrow in the heel.

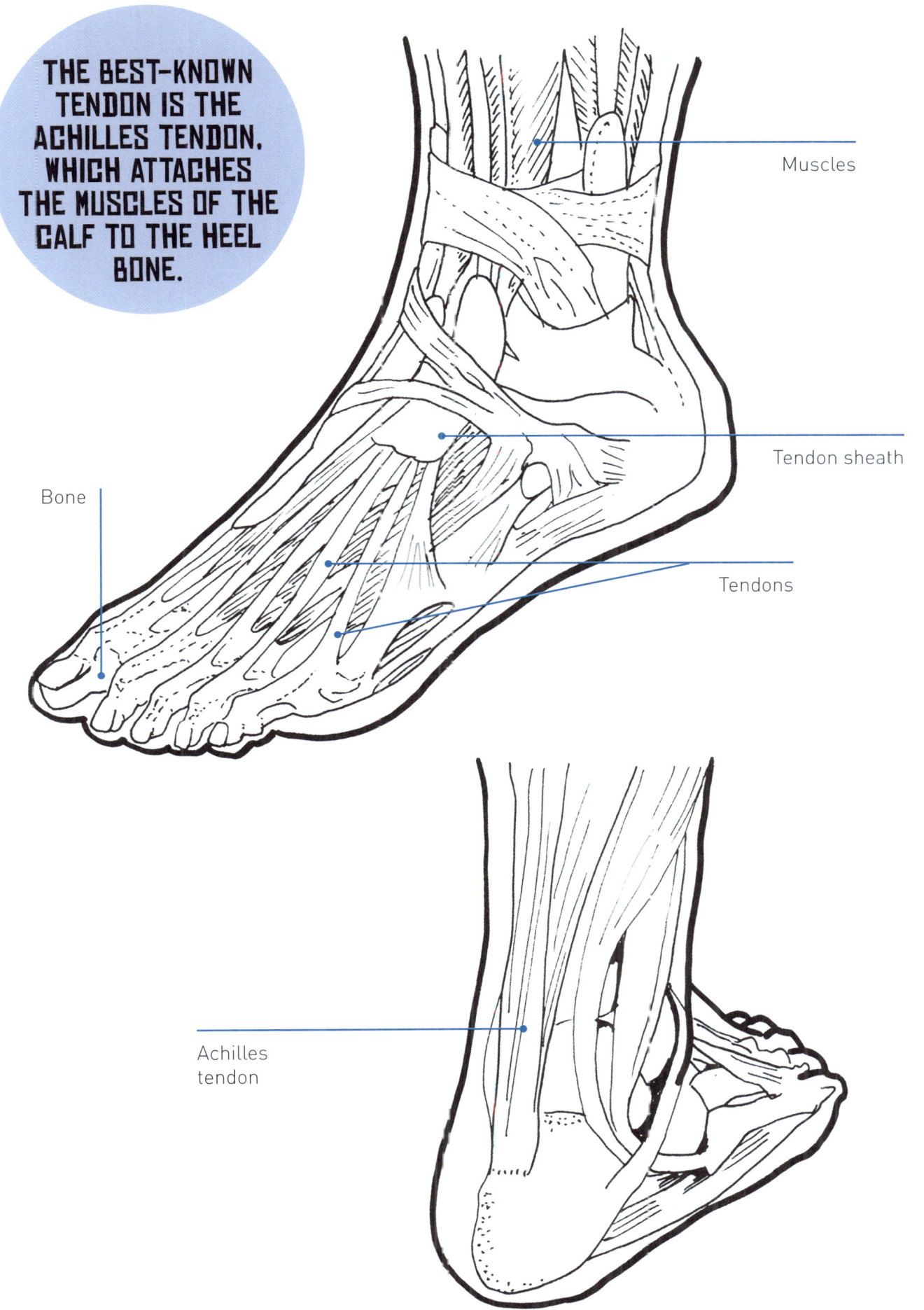

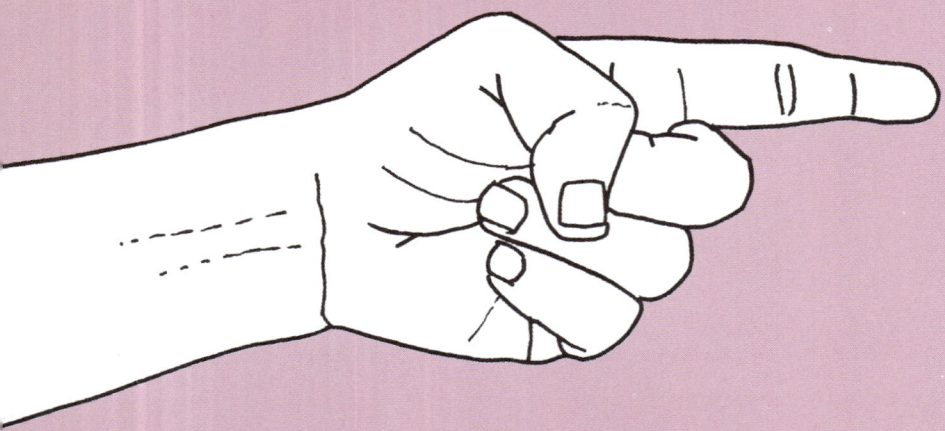

HANDS AND FEET

Your hands and feet have a similar bone structure.

The arrangement of the muscles in your hands and feet gives them great strength without making your fingers and toes so thick that they would be difficult to move.

QUICK FACTS

It takes 35 powerful **MUSCLES** to move the human hand—15 are in the forearm, rather than in the hand itself.

The human **FOOT** has 26 bones.

There are as many as 30 joint surfaces in the human **WRIST** and **HAND**.

The **ELBOW** is the joint that connects a person's upper arm with their forearm.

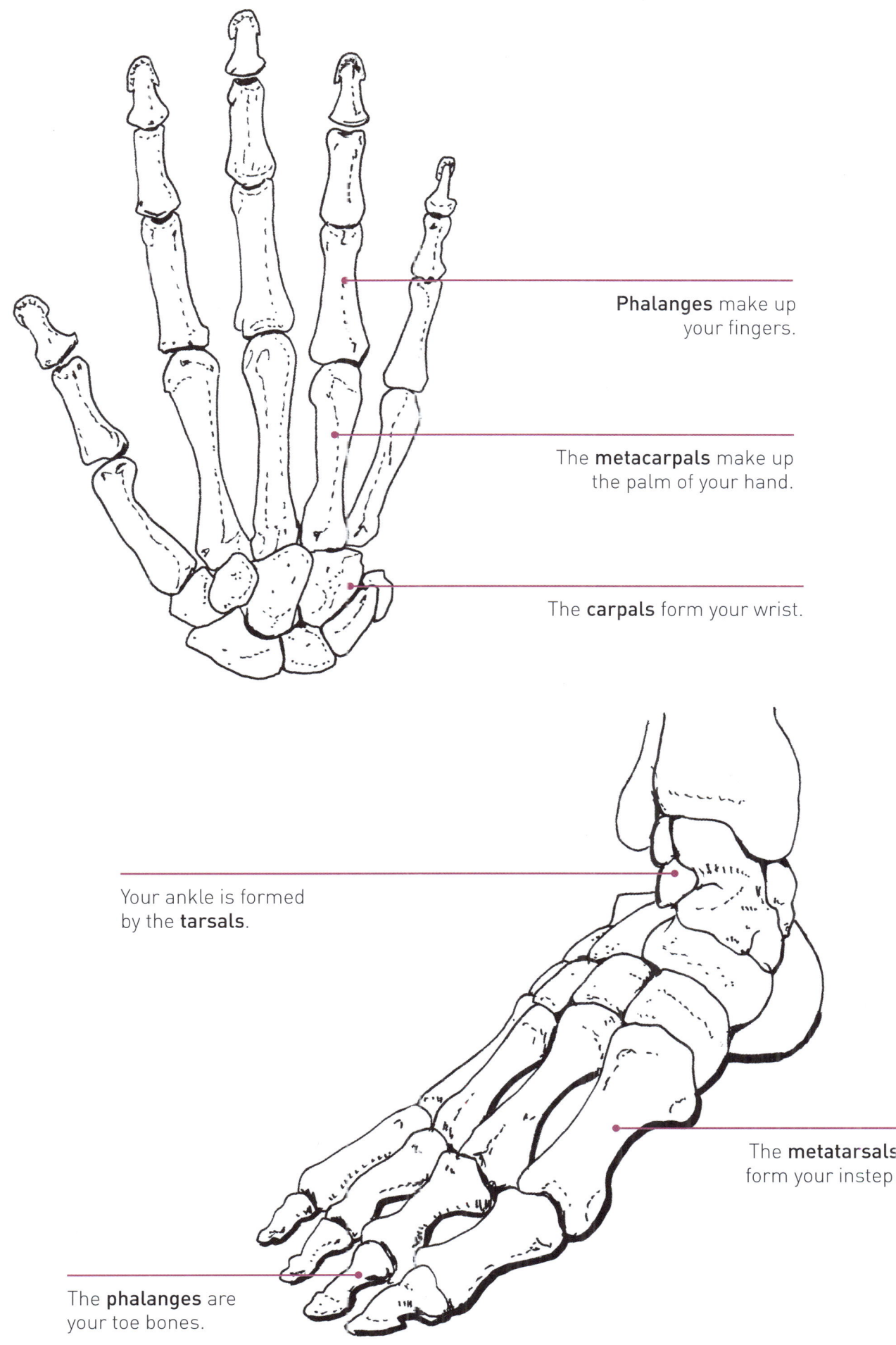

Phalanges make up your fingers.

The **metacarpals** make up the palm of your hand.

The **carpals** form your wrist.

Your ankle is formed by the **tarsals**.

The **metatarsals** form your instep.

The **phalanges** are your toe bones.

ARMS AND LEGS

The long bones of the arms and legs work like levers, with their pivot at the joint.

The knee joint is the largest and most complex joint in the body. It moves like a hinge, but it can also rotate and move a little from side to side.

QUICK FACTS

The **HUMERUS** is the body's largest bone. It's also the only bone in the upper arm.

The **PATELLA** (or kneecap) is a small, flat, triangular bone just in front of the joint.

The patella is not directly **CONNECTED** with any other bone. Muscle attachments hold it in place.

The knee **LIGAMENTS** are the strongest connections between the femur and the tibia. They prevent the bones moving out of position.

Soccer requires sturdy knees and ankles.

A tennis player must have huge muscular strength in her arms.

THE FLEXIBILITY OF OUR ARMS AND LEGS ALLOWS US TO MAKE THE KIND OF COMPLEX MOVEMENT REQUIRED FOR SPORTS.

A swimmer must be strong all over!

BONES 95

Look out for all three of the fantastic Colour + Learn titles:

Prehistoric World
Human Body
Science and Space

These amazing books all have over 90 pages of facts and colouring fun!